Hampton and Its Students

Hampton and Its Students
Prepared for publication
By
HISTORIC PULISHING
©2017 All rights reserved.

All edited images and edited written materials contained within are protected by copyright. No part of this publication may be reproduced, distributed, or transmitted in any form or by any means, including: photocopying, recording, or by any other electronic or mechanical methods without the express written consent of the author.

Hampton and Its Students
ISBN: 978-1-946640-21-5
All rights reserved.

Hampton
And its Students.
By
Two of its Teachers,
Mrs. M. F. Armstrong and Helen W. Ludlow.
With Fifty Cabin and Plantation Songs,
Arranged by Thomas P. Fenner

Armstrong, M. F. (Mary Frances), d.1903,
Helen W. Ludlow (Helen Wilhelmina), d. 1924 and Thomas P. Fenner

Young Women's Department, with Industrial and Dining Rooms.
[Virginia Hall stands just in rear of the above long wooden, building, which will eventually be removed.]
Teacher's Residence.
Hampton Creek.
Barn and Storehouse.
Young Men's Department, with Assembly and Recitation Rooms.
Hampton Normal and Agricultural Institute.
[BEFORE THE ERECTION OF VIRGINIA HALL.]

Hampton and Its Students

HAMPTON AND ITS STUDENTS.

BY

TWO OF ITS TEACHERS,

MRS. M. F. ARMSTRONG

AND

HELEN W. LUDLOW.

WITH FIFTY CABIN AND PLANTATION SONGS,

ARRANGED BY

THOMAS P. FENNER,

IN CHARGE OF MUSICAL DEPARTMENT AT HAMPTON.

> "I'm gwine to climb up higher and higher,
> I'm gwine to climb up higher and higher,
> I'm gwine to climb up higher and higher;
> Den my little soul's gwine to shine, shine,
> Oh! den my little soul's gwine to shine along."
> *Old Slave Song.*

NEW-YORK:
G. P. PUTNAM'S SONS.
1874.

HAMPTON AND ITS STUDENTS.

BY
TWO OF ITS TEACHERS,
MRS. M. F. ARMSTRONG
AND
HELEN W. LUDLOW.

WITH FIFTY CABIN AND PLANTATION SONGS,

ARRANGED BY
THOMAS P. FENNER,

IN CHARGE OF MUSICAL DEPARTMENT AT HAMPTON.

"I'm gwine to climb up higher and higher,
I'm gwine to climb up higher and higher,
I'm gwine to climb up higher and higher;
Den my little soul's gwine to shine, shine,
Oh! den my little soul's gwine to shine along."

Old Slave Song.

NEW-YORK:
G. P. PUTNAM'S SONS.
1874
Entered, according to Act of Congress, in the year 1874, by
HELEN W. LUDLOW,
in the Office of the Librarian of Congress, at Washington.

Hampton and Its Students

INTRODUCTION

The Hampton and its Students is a lost treasury of informative subject matter regarding race and education. Although, the book has a focus on education in a variety of facets, there are subject matters dealing with race relations that are invaluable.

PREFACE.

THE desire to know more about Hampton and its students, on the part of the many friends of this Institution, has been one reason for publishing this little book. To them, and to the many other friends of the freedmen and of all the great interests of humanity who, we hope, will be made Hampton's friends by reading it, the authors wish to say that while the impressions it gives of the school and the life in and around it are in every sense their own, for which they are therefore alone responsible, the historical and statistical information contained in these pages is official, and may be relied upon as accurate.

For all of its illustrations, except the first and the last three, the book is indebted to the courtesy of Messrs. Harper Bros., who have kindly allowed the use of their woodcuts.

M. F. A.
H. W. L.

HAMPTON, January 1, 1874.

CONTENTS.

- INTRODUCTION............................9
- PREFACE...............................10
- THE SCHOOL AND ITS STORY ..... *M. F. Armstrong*......14
- A TEACHER'S WITNESS ..... *M. F. Armstrong*......34
- THE BUTLER SCHOOL ..... *M. F. Armstrong*......58
- INTERIOR VIEWS OF THE SCHOOL AND THE CABIN. *Helen W. Ludlow* 63
- What is the Privileged Color?............65
- A Wolf in Sheep's Clothing..............66
- How Aunt Sally Hugged the Old Flag......69
- The Woman Question Again...............72
- The Richness of English................77
- The Sunny Side of Slavery..............80
- Father Parker's Story..................84
- "Want to feel right about it"..........89
- K. K. K...............................91
- A Case of Incomplete Sanctification.....93
- Just where to put dem..................99
- Hunger and Thirst after Knowledge.....104
- THE HAMPTON STUDENTS IN THE NORTH--SINGING AND BUILDING. *Helen W. Ludlow*..........108
- VIRGINIA HALL ..... *Helen W. Ludlow*..........131
- APPENDIX.............................139
- CABIN AND PLANTATION SONGS............159

Hampton and Its Students

LIST OF ILLUSTRATIONS.

- Hampton Normal and Agricultural Institute
- Virginia Hall
- Walls of St. John's Church
- Teachers' Home and Girls' Quarters
- Chapel and Farm Manager's Home
- Lion and John Solomon
- Printing-Office
- Girls' Industrial Room
- Assembly-Room
- Reading-Room
- Winter Quarters
- Ball Club
- Butler School-House
- Negro Cabin at Hampton
- Virginia Hall--New Building
- Virginia Hall--Second-floor Plan
- Virginia Hall--Interior of Girls' Room

THE SCHOOL AND ITS STORY.

By M. F. A.

AMONG all the States of the Union, not one has a history more interesting than Virginia, for her annals are full of strangely poetic incident, from the world-famous idyll of Pocahontas to the tragic stories still fresh in our own memories; and from the fertile seaboard to the rich mountain valleys of her western border, there is scarcely a field or village that has not its tale to tell. More than one great name, "familiar in our mouths as household words," belongs in the catalogue of Virginia's children; and although to-day her greatness is a thing of the past and the future, yet that future promises such certainty as is more than guaranteed by her natural advantages and the brave and willing temper of her people.

In the history of this State, there arose, long years ago, an unnatural relation between two races, which furnished a problem, dealt with by statesmen, philanthropists, and fanatics, and finally solved by God himself, in his own time, and his own way; and it is with an outgrowth of that problem and its solution that this little book has to do.

The introduction of negroes into the country as slaves was made at a time when only a few minds, here and there, had any true conception of the rights of individuals, or could put a fair interpretation upon that higher law which makes us our brothers' keepers; and the virgin soil and relaxing climate of the South made slavery so temptingly easy and profitable as to insure its continuance until a Power stronger than humanity interfered to bring it to an end. In no part of the United States can the history of negro slavery, from its origin to its extinction, be more clearly traced than in Virginia; and as that State was chosen as the scene of bitterest struggle, so it seems likely to attain the earliest and highest development, for within its borders are now being fairly tested the possibilities of, the African race, and the results to them and the whites of the new relations of freedom. It is not too much to say that throughout the history of slavery in Virginia, there runs a strain of poetic justice, which is absolutely dramatic, robbing facts of their dryness and interweaving the prosaic details of life with the elements of tragedy. Nowhere has there been greater prosperity, nowhere has there been greater suffering, and many a page might be filled with the record of the changes which a century has wrought, of the old things that have passed away, and the new hopes that are blossoming for the future; and in writing this brief story of an experiment which is just now being tried upon Virginian soil, there will be an earnest attempt to offer such testimony of the capacity of a hitherto enslaved race, and of the intelligent and generous action of their whilom owners, as shall not be altogether valueless.

Hampton and Its Students

THE HAMPTON INSTITUTE--THE NEW BUILDING, VIRGINIA HALL.

This experiment of negro education is too serious a matter to be treated otherwise than with the severest honesty; it is not to be wrought out in the white heat of fanaticism, or the glow of a superficial sentiment, but must rather be tested by patient, practical trial on the largest possible scale; and such trial can at present be made only under specially favorable circumstances. There must be a suitable climate, a need and an ability to pay for skilled labor, and a fairly unprejudiced and intelligent white population, while, of course, the willingness of the blacks themselves to assist in the work of their own enlightenment must, to a certain extent, be taken for granted. Such a combination of circumstances exists in a marked degree in Virginia, and in that State, past events seem, in a curious fashion, to have paved the way for the present endeavor. Not but that what may be found true of the blacks in Virginia will hold good in all parts of our Southern country, but merely that in all initial experiments of this nature, involving possibly the life of a whole race, justice demands that the weakness and ignorance of those whose fate hangs in the balance should, if possible, be compensated for by the offer of especial opportunities.

Therefore, when we ask our readers to go back with us at first into the past of a little Virginian town, we are only asking them to trace by and by for themselves a logical sequence of events whose results promise to-day a glorious success, and whose close relation to each other can scarcely be without interest to any who are taking thought as to the future of the African people on this continent. We have said that there is scarcely a village in Virginia that has not its tale to tell, and truly no romancer need desire richer material than lies ready to his hand in many of the older settlements which still bear the mark of their English origin, and hold in their moldy parish-registers or upon the moss-grown stones in their neglected graveyards, the names of famous old English houses whose cadets, or even whose heads, came with rash enterprise to meet their death in the wilderness which they dreamed was to yield them instead a fabulous treasure.

Just at the mouth of the Chesapeake Bay, where one of its numerous tributary creeks opens into the broad harbor of Hampton Roads, stands a little village, scattered along the western shore of the creek, with its half-ruined houses and low, white cabins irregularly clustered upon the level green meadows down to the very water's edge. The back country through which the creek wanders for the few miles of its course, and the shore itself, are flat and monotonous, except for the brilliant coloring and golden, semi-tropical sunshine, which for eight months in the year redeem the landscape from the latter charge. But the changeful beauty of the shore, even when at its climax in the fresh spring months, can bear no comparison with the eternal beauty of the sea, which, stretching far on either hand, offers by day and night, in calm and storm, new glories and beautiful, strange surprises of color and sound and motion. When the fury of an Atlantic storm drives vessel after vessel into the secure anchorage of the Roads, until a whole fleet is gathered under the guns of Old Point Comfort; or when, on some bright, breezy morning, scores of white-winged oyster-boats put out from every safe nook of the shore, dotting the sparkling blue of the bay like snowy birds; or, better still, when the fading crimson glow of sunset makes the shore shadowy and indistinct, and the little returning flotilla floats tranquilly homeward to the slow dip of oars and the weird, rich singing of the negro boatmen--then one gazes and listens, to confess at last that such scenes are hard to rival, and that this unfamiliar bit of Virginia coast need not fear the verdict of critics with whom still lingers the remembrance of Mediterranean skies or distant tropic seas.

By this broad, shining sea-path, there came, more than two hundred years ago, the daring little band of Englishmen who settled the town of Hampton, and made it their headquarters in the colonization of the neighboring country. Their story is too well known to every child in America to need recapitulation here. Their hopes and their disappointments, their struggles and sufferings, their defeats, and final victory over the obstacles that opposed their determination to possess, in their Queen's name, the beautiful fertile land they had discovered-- all these are a part of the nation's history not easily to be forgotten. In Hampton itself still stands the quaint little church of St. John, built between 1660 and 1667, and the records of the court, which date as far back as 1635, prove that even before that time a church had been built; while the old, deserted graveyard has many a grave whose hollow holds the dust of English hearts broken or wearied out by unaccustomed hardship. Here and there may still be found vestiges of these earliest occupants of the soil; but from its first settlement, the town of Hampton has passed through such vicissitude as does not often fall to the lot of an obscure village; for the fortunes of war have been uniformly against it, and it has seen more wars than one. In 1812, the town was sacked and left desolate, its geographical position exposing it to especial dangers, while it was unable to defend itself, and was not of sufficient importance to receive efficient protection.

WALLS OF ST. JOHN'S CHURCH.

    Years before this time, however, the curse which was the cause of the blighted prosperity, not of one town only, but of the whole South, had fallen, and when the first cargo of slaves was landed within a few miles of Hampton, it was as if men's eyes were thereafter blinded to the light of God's truth, for from that hapless day, each year but added to the incubus, until relief could only come through fire and sword. Viewed in the light of later events, this landing of the first slaves at Hampton ranks as one of the strange coincidences of fate; for here upon the spot where they tasted first the bitterness of slavery, they also first attained to the privileges of freemen, the famous order which made them "contraband of war," and thereby virtually gave them their freedom, having been issued by General Benjamin F. Butler, from the camp at Fortress Monroe, in May, 1861.

The year of 1861 opened with threats of trouble near at hand, and before the spring had fairly set in, our civil war began, the country in the neighborhood of Fortress Monroe becoming almost immediately the scene of bitter contest; for the importance of that post as a Centre of operations was second to none other on the Atlantic seaboard. The creek upon which Hampton stands was for a while the boundary-line between the two armies--the Union lines remaining entrenched upon its eastern shore during the early part of the war, while the combating forces swayed back and forth, as fortune favored one or the other. The town and the long bridge across the creek were burned, and the few houses of the richer residents, which escaped the general destruction, were made the headquarters of Union or Confederate officers, as might be, until the lawless hands of successive possessors had obliterated all traces of former luxury. Before the war, Hampton and Old Point Comfort were favorite watering-places with the better class of Virginians, and summer after summer had seen the rambling, airy houses filled with Southern aristocracy; so that the havoc of war wrought a quick and startling change from the gayety of one season to the terror of the next.

But as the months went by, a greater change than all drew near; and when in the early summer of 1861, troops of blacks came pouring in from the interior of the State and the northern counties of North-Carolina, then, indeed, the real meaning of the war and its inevitable end became apparent, and the question was no longer, "What is to be done with the slaves?" but instead, "What is to be done with the freedmen?"

Newbern, North Carolina, and Hampton, Virginia, were the two cities of refuge to which they fled, their lives in their hands, as the Israelites of old fled from the avengers of blood. Fortress Monroe and its guns offered tangible protection, and the spirit of the officers in command promised a surer protection still; so that in little squads, in families, singly, or by whole plantations, the negroes flocked within the Northern lines, until the whole area of ground protected by the Union encampments was crowded with their little hurriedly-built cabins of rudely-split logs. A remnant of these still remains in a suburb of Hampton, numbering about five hundred inhabitants, and known by the significant name of Slabtown, and another called more euphoniously Sugar Hill--on some principle of lucus a non lucendo, it must be, as it is situated on a dead level, and certainly has no appearance of offering much literal or figurative sweetening to the lives of its inhabitants.

Hampton and Its Students

How these people lived was and still is a mystery, for the rations issued them from the army and hospital establishment were necessarily insufficient, and those at the North who would gladly have welcomed the newcomers with practical assistance were already overburdened with the paramount claims of army work. However, all through that long first summer of the war, we find occasional evidence that these newborn children of freedom were not altogether forgotten; and in October of the same year, we know that organized work was begun among them.

This work was initiated by the officers of the American Missionary Association, who, in August, 1861, sent down as missionary to the freedmen, the Rev. C. L. Lockwood, his way having been opened for him by an official correspondence and interviews with the Assistant Secretary of War and Generals Butler and Wool, all of whom heartily approved of the enterprise and offered him cordial cooperation. He found the "contrabands" quartered in deserted houses, in cabins and tents, destitute and desolate, but in the main willing to help themselves as far as possible, and of at least average intelligence and honesty. There was, of course, little regular employment to offer them, and they subsisted upon government rations, increased by the little they could earn in one way and another. Mr. Lockwood's first work was the establishment of Sunday-schools and church societies, and his own words show the spirit in which the assistance he was able to give was offered and received. He says, in one of his first letters to the American Missionary Association, "I shall mingle largely with my religious instruction the inculcation of industrious habits, order, and good conduct in every respect. I tell them that they are a spectacle before God and man, and that if they would further the cause of liberty; it behooves them to be impressed with their own responsibility. I am happy to find that they realize this to a great extent already."

This was certainly encouraging, and he goes on to report that he finds little intemperance, and a hunger for books among those who can read, which is most gratifying. He appeals at once for primers, and for two or three female teachers to open weekday schools; and recommends that, in view of the imperativeness of the need, the subject should be brought before the public through the daily press and by means of public meetings. At the same time, he describes the opening of the first Sunday school in the deserted mansion of ex-President Tyler, in Hampton, and, from his personal observation, declares that many of the colored people are kept away from the schools by want of clothing, a want which he looks to the North to supply. A little later in the year, he writes that, on November 17th, the first day-school was opened with twenty scholars and a colored teacher, Mrs. Peake, who, before the war, being free herself, had privately instructed many of her people who were still enslaved, although such work was not without its dangers.

Hampton and Its Students

From this time, schools were established as rapidly as suitable teachers could be found and proper books provided; but it must be noted that these teachers were working almost *without compensation*, their sole motive being a desire for the elevation of the race. As a proof of the quick awakening of the ex-slaves to a sense of the duties of freedom, Mr. Lockwood mentions that marriages were becoming very frequent, and that although the fugitives lived in constant fear of being remanded to slavery, they did not remit their efforts to obtain education and to raise themselves from the degradation of their past.

In December, 1861, at the annual meeting of the American Missionary Association, it was resolved that "the new field of missionary labor in Virginia should be faithfully cultivated, and that the colored brethren there were fully entitled to the advantages of compensated labor;" which latter clause was a much-needed acknowledgment, for in the same month we find it stated that government, in return for the rations supplied to the freedmen around Fortress Monroe, claimed the labor of all who were able to work, giving them a nominal payment, the greater part of which was retained by the quartermasters for the use of the women, children, and infirm. The honesty and wisdom with which this provision was apportioned depended, of course, upon the character of the quartermasters and their interest in the people; and there is do doubt that even when the administration was thoroughly just, the supply was entirely inadequate to the need. In accordance with the above resolution, the American Missionary Association increased the number of their colored employees, and, in January, 1862, sent down a second reinforcement of missionaries and teachers-- the reports of the progress of the negroes and their eagerness for knowledge continuing remarkably favorable, while the devotion of a few was worthy of a more public acknowledgment than it has ever received; as, for example, Mrs. Peake, who died in April, 1862, having literally laid down her life for her people, for whom she labored beyond her strength until death lifted her self-imposed burden.

During all these months, the attention of the Northern public had been gradually attracted toward the condition of the freedmen at various points throughout the South, and, on the 20th of February, 1862, a great meeting was held in the Cooper Institute, New-York, at which many prominent men were present, and a committee appointed who organized themselves as the "National Freedmen's Relief Association," and announced their desire "to work, with the cooperation of the Federal Government, for the relief and improvement of the freedmen of the colored race; to teach them civilization and Christianity; to imbue them with notions of order, industry, economy, and self-reliance; and to elevate them in the scale of humanity by inspiring them with self-respect." This meeting gave incontrovertible evidence of the rapidity with which sympathy for the freedmen had grown up in the North; but at the same time this sympathy was as yet, necessarily, of a very general character, and, indeed, it was not then possible to enter into details, for the great fact of the permanent emancipation of the slaves was not yet fully established, and innumerable difficulties beset those who undertook any systematized effort for their relief. Complaints had been made in regard to the treatment of those at Fortress Monroe, and General Wool had appointed a committee to examine into their condition, moral and physical, which commission, after a faithful discharge of their duty, reported on most points favorably--making, however, some suggestions as to future action, the principal of which was the recommendation that the government should appoint some responsible civil agent to the charge of the improvement of the freedmen. Captain C. B. Wilder, of Boston, was appointed superintendent of their affairs, and rendered efficient service in their behalf.

Mr. Lockwood still held his position as missionary to Hampton, and in July of this year wrote that the building of small tenements was going on rapidly, gardens were being cultivated, while a church and school-house were finished and occupied; and one of the officers of the American Missionary Association reported, on his return from a tour of inspection, that the general evidences of improvement were most satisfactory. Undoubtedly, the quick and generous reply of the North to the demand made upon their beneficence had much to do with the safe transition of the blacks from slavery to freedom; but it must be remembered that opinion in the North was still divided, and that more was due to the patient, determined spirit of the freedmen themselves than to any other cause, A noteworthy exhibition of this spirit occurred shortly after the decision of the officers of the "Freedmen's Bureau," that no more rations were to be issued to the blacks about Fortress Monroe, at a time when a large number of them had no visible means of support except such as government furnished. The distribution of rations ceased abruptly upon a certain day, October 1st, 1866,* and the expectation of the officers stationed at Hampton was that there would ensue general and probably serious disturbance in the crowded quarters of the colored people, who must necessarily feel the deprivation very acutely. On the contrary, the report of these officers is, that the order was carried out without producing the smallest expression of dissatisfaction, and the usual tranquility was maintained. The two thousand freedmen who had been fed by government for years, and were living in the depths of poverty answered almost at once the sudden and severe draught upon their resources, and proved themselves possessors of unsuspected strength.

*See Appendix, Note i.

Hampton and Its Students

Ignorant as these people were, they knew that they were free, and in no way did they mean to trifle with their newfound blessing. They had a curiously quick appreciation of the fact that freedom meant little to them unless they knew how to use it, and they discerned for themselves that their primary need was education. After the President's proclamation, published in October, 1862, the demand for schools steadily increased, and as the opportunities for their safe establishment and support increased also, there began an amelioration of the condition of the freedmen, which promised to be permanent because based on a sure foundation. The physical destitution was so great that no charity, however broad, could do more, than afford superficial relief, and it soon became evident that, on every account, the best help for these people was that which soonest taught them to help themselves. Untrained as they were, even in respect to the simplest facts of life, their education had at the outset to be, of necessity, of the most elementary character, and such primary schools as could with comparative ease be supplied with both teachers and books amply sufficed, and for the first two or three years seemed to the blacks like the gates of heaven. As the number of fugitives near Hampton grew from month to month, and the prospect was that for many of them the settlement there would become a permanent home, these primary schools increased in number and capacity, one of them alone receiving within three months more than eight hundred scholars, while night-schools and Sunday-schools took in many who for various reasons could not attend during the usual day-school hours.

The Society of Friends at the North had, early in the war, shown great interest in the freedmen, had sent several teachers to Hampton and the vicinity, and was at this time occupying one of the deserted houses as an Orphan Asylum. These teachers worked in hearty cooperation with the teachers of the American Missionary Association, and the little band struggled bravely with the gigantic undertaking, for the work at this point, where there were not less than 1600 pupils, was growing so rapidly that failure here was especially to be dreaded.

But no teachers of another race could do for the freed people what was waiting to be done by men and women of their own blood. In 1866, the American Missionary Association determined upon the opening of a normal school, and in January, 1867, there appeared in the *American Missionary Magazine* an article by General S. C. Armstrong, earnestly and ably setting forth the need of normal schools for colored people, wherein they could be trained as teachers, and fitted to take up the work of civilizing their expectant brethren; and this article was followed later in the year by reports from various well-qualified employees of the American Missionary Association as to the feasibility of this scheme. They were unanimous in their approval, and strongly urged the necessity of immediate action, recommending the establishment of normal or training schools as soon as adequate funds could be procured.

Hampton and Its Students

As is evident from the foregoing sketch of the growth of the work at Hampton, everything pointed to that place as of primary importance; for, here was collected one of the largest settlements of fugitives (the population being of greater relative density than at any other point on the Atlantic coast), here was a central and healthy situation, and here was protection and a close connection with the sympathies of the Northern public. Furthermore--and herein the thought of God seems too clear for us to dare to speak of it as "chance"--the chief official of the Freedmen's Bureau at Hampton was at this time General S. C. Armstrong, late Colonel of the Eighth Regiment U. S. Colored Troops and Brigadier-General by Brevet, whose interest in the blacks was earnest and practical, and whose peculiar preparation for the work before him has had so much to do with the results of that work, that it cannot be passed over unnoticed.

General Armstrong is the son of the Rev. Richard Armstrong, D.D., who for nearly forty years was missionary to the Sandwich Islands. It may be interesting, in connection with his son's work in Virginia, to know that Dr. Armstrong received his doctorate from Washington College, Lexington, Va., with whose President, Rev. Dr. Junkin, he was an intimate friend at Carlisle College, Pa.

During sixteen years of his long life as missionary, Dr. Armstrong was Minister of Public Instruction of the Hawaiian Kingdom, and in that, position largely influenced the policy of the government in respect to the school system of the Islands. He succeeded in establishing the higher schools upon a manual-labor basis, and these schools have been and still are remarkably satisfactory, both pecuniarily and in the character and efficiency of their graduates. Dr. Armstrong's life as a public man was one of incessant labor, and in the sphere of usefulness which he may be said to have created, his son was trained until his twenty-first year, when, after having served actively in the Department of Public Instruction at Honolulu for one year, he was sent into the stimulating atmosphere of a New-England college, to complete his education, at Williamstown, Mass. Graduating from Williams College in the summer of 1862, he at once entered the army as captain in a New-York regiment, shortly afterward received a commission in the U. S. Colored Troops, and as colonel of a colored regiment, gained an experience of the negro in a military capacity, which at the close of the war was supplemented by a term of service in the Freedmen's Bureau, where he became thoroughly familiar with the civil needs of the newly-made citizens.

Trained by this rare combination of events, General Armstrong, placed in a position of power at Hampton, seized at once the salient points of the situation, and found himself, from very force of habit, in quick sympathy with the people for whom he was called upon to act. Thenceforward, the key-note of the work of which we write was found in the fact that its chief brought from Hawaii to Virginia an idea, worked out by

Hampton and Its Students

American brains in the heart of the Pacific, adequate to meet the demands of a race similar in its dawn of civilization to the people among whom this idea had first been successfully tested.

General Armstrong saw that the need of the freedmen, now that their escape from slavery had become a certainty, was a training which should as swiftly as possible redeem their past and fit them for the demands that a near future was to make upon them. They needed not only the teaching of books, but the far broader teaching of a free and yet disciplined life, and the surest way to convince them of their own capacity for the duties imposed upon them by freedom was to show them members of their own race trained to self-respect, industry, and real practical virtue. Teachers of their own race must be had, young men and women, who could go out among them, and, as the heads of primary schools, could control and lead the children, while, by the influence of their orderly, intelligent lives, they could at the same time substantially affect the moral and physical condition of the parents. Normal schools upon the broadest plan were the thing required; and as the American Missionary Association, who, by right of their earnest labor, were in possession of the field at Hampton, were favorably inclined to such an experiment, General Armstrong resolved, with their cooperation and at their request, to devote himself to the work of founding a manual-labor school for colored people, from which should go forth not only school-teachers, but farm teachers, home-teachers, teachers of practical Christianity, bearing with them to their work at least some faint reflection of the spirit of Christ himself. What could be more natural, more beautiful than the growth of such a school within the lines of Camp Hamilton, close to the spot sullied by the footsteps of the first slaves, on the very ground where the first freedmen's school was opened, and where, when the Monitor and the Merrimac met yonder in the blue water of the "Roads," a crowd of dusky figures was gathered in piteous, imploring prayer that victory might not be unto the foe, whose success meant the old terror, the awful darkness, of human bondage.

Here then should rise, God willing, the walls of such a building as America had never seen, a building whose corner-stone should be the freedom of Christianity, and from whose gates should go out, year after year, men and women fitted for righteous labor among a people whose past is a blot upon the national honor, staining the escutcheons of both North and South, and to whom North and South, alike owe a debt to be repaid only by wise and liberal care for many a day to come.

So, in the midst of suffering, in the midst of dangers and uncertainties, with no sure promise of support, the school began its life, and inaugurated its work in April, 1868, being incorporated by the General Assembly of Virginia, in June, 1870, as the "*Hampton Normal and Agricultural Institute*," with the following Board of Trustees:

President, George Whipple, New-York; Vice-Presidents, R. W. Hughes, Abingdon, Va.; Alexander Hyde, Lee, Mass.; Secretary, S. C. Armstrong, Hampton, Va.; Financial Secretary, Thomas K. Fessenden, Farmington, Ct.; Treasurer, J. F. B. Marshall, Boston, Mass.; O. O. Howard, Washington, D. C.; M. E. Strieby, Newark, N. J.; James A. Garfield, Hiram, Ohio; E. P. Smith, Washington, D. C.; John F. Lewis, Port Republic, Va.; B. G. Northrop, New-Haven, Ct.; Samuel Holmes, Montclair, N. J.; Anthony M. Kimber, Philadelphia, Pa.; Edgar Ketchum, New-York City; E. M. Cravath, Brooklyn, N. Y.; H. C. Percy, Norfolk, Va.; who now hold and control the entire property of the Institute, and to whose wisdom is due the adoption of the carefully elaborated system which experience has proved to be so successful.

Little by little, the building grew; money and helping hands came from the North; a hundred acres of good farm-land gave opportunity for that practical education in agriculture so sadly needed throughout the South; and although the struggle was unceasing, the spirit of those on whom the burden fell never for a moment flagged, and the work went steadily on. One by one, friends were made who pledged themselves that "Hampton" should not fail; and the wisdom and experience of more than one co-laborer were placed at General Armstrong's disposal. With the hearty generosity characteristic of him, General O. O. Howard, both as head of the Freedmen's Bureau and as a private individual, gave good help again and again to the school which was to do a work after his own heart, and from the date of its opening to the present day, he has proved an unfailing friend and benefactor.[*] *See Appendix, Note 2.
As the plan of the school became more generally understood, students flocked in, not from Virginia alone, but from many States of the South, and showed an appreciation of the opportunity offered them greater than the most hopeful of the laborers among them had dared to expect. The corps of teachers was necessarily enlarged, and a "Home" furnished for them in one of the houses purchased with the farm, while a long line of deserted barracks and a second building, formerly used as a grist-mill, were taken for girls' dormitories--these, with the necessary barns and workshops, all standing in convenient neighborhood to each other, close down upon the shore, completing the present list of school-buildings.

TEACHER'S HOME AND GIRL'S QUARTERS.

The history of the school from the time of its legal organization until today is the history of a brave struggle against opposing circumstances, which has been made thus far successful by the determined spirit of students and teachers, the steady liberality of Northern friends, and the generosity of Virginia. In recalling the list of those who have fed the growth of the school with full and cheerful bounty, it is almost impossible to avoid the mention of special names and instances, and yet in any such mention it is inevitable that much must be left unsaid and the story of many a gracious deed remain untold. There is perhaps no feature of the history of Hampton more striking and more valuable as a proof of the power of unity of purpose than the fact that the school is, as it claims to be, truly un-sectarian, and that while founded by the American Missionary Association, and therefore strictly orthodox in its origin and evangelical in its teaching, it ranks among its supporters and warm friends, Quakers, Unitarians, societies and men of every shade of belief.

The gift which gave Hampton its first impetus came in the spring of 1867, when the Hon. Josiah King, one of the executors of the "Avery Fund," of Pittsburg, Pa., visited Hampton, and decided to expend, through the Association, $10,000 of that legacy in assisting to purchase the "Wood Farm" or "Little Scotland," a tract of land on the east side of the creek, known during the war as Camp Hamilton, in which, at one time, as many as fifteen thousand sick and wounded Union soldiers have been cared for. This property consisted of 125 acres of excellent land, besides two outlying lots of small value, containing 40 acres, with some $12,000 worth of available buildings, and the total cost was $19,000, of which the American Missionary Association paid $9000, thus holding the property until the appointment of the Board of Trustees, whose names have already been given, to whom the property and control of the school were transferred in 1872.

As a natural result of military occupancy, the farm was at this time entirely out of condition, and both buildings and soil required an immediate and comparatively large outlay. The Freedmen's Bureau made an appropriation of about $2000 to aid with the buildings, and just as this was exhausted, and the position most critical, Mrs. Stephen Griggs, of New York, made a timely gift of $6000, increasing it afterward to $10,000, which put the institution on a firm foundation. From time to time, General Howard, as chief of the Freedmen's Bureau, granted additional funds for building and other purposes, amounting to upward of $50,000, and contributions of from $50 to $500 dropped in from various sources, increasing as the school grew, and furnishing so sure a supply, that, although the treasury was at times absolutely empty, and the coming of the next dollar an entire uncertainty, yet, in obedience to some unknown law of supply and demand, the next dollar never failed to come and save the school from a bankruptcy which was more than once threatened. Thus, when the present Academic Hall had been completed, at a cost of $48,000, and $44,500 was all that the most strenuous efforts had been able to secure, a generous lady of Boston canceled the debt. And now again, when the recent panic in the money market had caused the income of resources for the building of Virginia Hall to cease entirely, two Boston friends guaranteed the funds for completing the walls and putting on the roof--a gift of about $10,000. Experiences like this cannot fail to strengthen our faith that this is God's work, and will go on in the future as it has in the past.

In 1872, the school received its first aid from Virginia, which was bestowed on it in its character as an agricultural college, and acknowledged as follows by the Board of Trustees at a meeting held in Hampton, June 12th, 1872:

"*Resolved* 1. That the trustees of the Hampton Normal and Agricultural Institute accept the trust reposed in them by the General Assembly of Virginia, in the act approved March 19th, 1872, entitled, 'An Act to appropriate the income arising from the proceeds of the land scrip accruing to Virginia under act of Congress of July 2d, 1862, and the acts amendatory thereof, on the terms and conditions therein set forth.'

"*Resolved*, 2. That, in view of this appropriation, the trustees hereby stipulate to establish at once a department in which thorough instruction shall be given, by carefully selected professors, in the following branches, namely, Practical Farming and Principles of Farming; Practical Mechanics and Principles of Mechanics; Chemistry, with special reference to Agriculture; Mechanical Drawing and Book-keeping; Military Tactics.

"*Resolved*, 3. That the trustees request leave of the curators to invest, at an early day, not more than one tenth of the principal of the land fund assigned to this institution in additional lands, to be used for farm purposes, and to expend not exceeding five hundred dollars ($500) during the present year in purchasing a chemical laboratory.

"*Resolved*, 4. That the Principal of this institution be authorized to receive one hundred students from the free colored schools of this State, free of charge, for instruction and use of public buildings, to be selected by him, in such manner as may, be agreed upon between himself and the Board of Education of the State of Virginia."

The appropriation was 100,000 acres of the public land scrip, sold in the market for $95,000, one tenth of which was expended for seventy acres of additional land, and the balance invested in State bonds bearing six per cent interest.

This noble gift is worthy of Virginia's advanced position in the work of development and progress before the South,[*] *See Governor Walker's letter, Appendix, Note 5. a position to which her Superintendent of Public Instruction, Dr. Win. H. Ruffner, points with just pride in his last deeply interesting report to the General Assembly. She is not only at the head of all the Southern States in the work of education, by her numerous colleges and universities, by her splendid school systems of Richmond and Petersburg, and her general and generous provision for common schools throughout the State, but it is proven by statistics that "where the white population alone is concerned, Virginia has a larger proportion of her sons in superior institutions probably than any State or country in the world." "What stronger evidence," Dr. Ruffner justly asks, "could be presented of the love of Virginia for the higher branches of learning than the fact that it cannot be quenched or even partially suppressed by the pinching poverty which now over-spreads the South?" It is evident that, as he told us last summer, at Hampton commencement, "our old State has entered honestly and uncomplainingly upon the work of educating her people, white and colored, with impartiality, and to the extent of her ability, *and she intends to keep on with it*."

The curators mentioned in the above resolutions are nine in number, five of whom are appointed by the Governor every fourth year, and it is provided that three of these five must be colored men. The State Board of Education, composed of the Governor, Attorney-General, and State Superintendent of Education, together with the President of the Virginia Agricultural Society, are curator's ex-officio.

Hampton and Its Students

The full Board consists at present of Gilbert C. Walker,[*] *By the last election of November, 1873; General James L. Kemper was elected Governor of Virginia, and becomes President, ex-officio, of the Board of Curators.
Governor of Virginia, President of the Board of Education; James E. Taylor, Attorney General; William H. Ruffner, Superintendent of Public Instruction; William H. F. Lee, President Virginia Agricultural Society. (The above named are ex-officio members.)

Appointed for a term of four years: O. M. Dorman, of Norfolk, Va.; Thomas Tabb, of Hampton, Va.; William Thornton, of Hampton, Va.; James H. Holmes, of Richmond, Va.; Caesar Perkins, of Buckingham C. H., Va.

This body of curators meet the trustees annually for the transaction of business, the last annual meeting bringing together a remarkable group of men of two races and opposing sentiment, who united in complete amity for a work of which they, one and all, appreciated the importance.[+] +See Appendix, Note 8.

This spirit of amity, of mutual respect, and good-will which has been constantly developing between the school and its Southern neighbors in the State and the town has been indeed one of the most gratifying and encouraging features in its history, and a most essential element in its success. Abundant evidence of the existence of such a spirit is found in the fact that from many of the best citizens of Hampton, the school has received friendly visits and frequent words of encouragement and good-will. One of her most eminent citizens is a member of the State Board of Curators of the Institute, and as its legal adviser, has rendered valuable and gratuitous service. To one of her leading clergymen, the school is indebted for interesting and instructive lectures, and for words of Christian sympathy and friendly counsel. One of her principal physicians has offered his services gratuitously to the school. More than one merchant of the town has made a liberal discount from his bill against it, and one, in doing so, adds these kind words:

"Please accept this as my humble mite toward the support of your admirable institution. Would that my means were such as to justify a more liberal discount."

All these instances of good-will, and others, which could be named, have come from citizens whose fortunes were cast with the South, in the late civil contest, and it is a pleasure to receive such proofs of their appreciation of the real aim and scope of the work. The distrust and occasional disfavor with which the enterprise was first viewed by some of them have gradually given place to confidence and good-will as time has developed its workings and its influence, and there is now between the school and its neighbors generally a mutual feeling of pleasure in each other's prosperity.

Hampton and Its Students

The growing prosperity of the town of Hampton, since its desolation by the war, is indeed a matter for rejoicing. Romantic as has been the tragic history of its past, it is by no means interesting merely as a ruin, but, on the contrary, is recovering itself with a rapidity that is striking and significant. The "contraband" tide, which overwhelmed it in 1861, in ebbing, left a residue behind which makes its population (2500) still nearly three quarters negro, but the condition of the freedmen, then greatly demoralized, has constantly improved. Five years ago, the trustees of the Normal School appropriated a portion of its lands for the erection of model cottages, which were sold to the freedmen at paying prices.

The ambition to become landowners, encouraged in this and in other ways, has so increased among them, that, as an intelligent white citizen of Hampton recently remarked, "not one of them is satisfied now till he owns a house and lot, and a cow. All the money he can get he saves up to buy them." A striking sign of the improvement in the relations of the freedman with his white neighbors is the fact that one of the principal proprietors of land in Hampton, one of its old residents, has recently been selling off his lots successively to white and colored bidders as they chanced to present themselves.

The army of slab huts, which once overran the desolated streets, has retreated to an outpost, which it still holds, but is gradually melting away before the advancing forces of civilization.

The town itself is steadily rising from its ashes. It has some fifty stores, a new and well-kept hotel, while the ancient walls of St. John's Church, which have withstood so many of the shocks of time, no longer stand in picturesque ruin, but gather within them every Sunday many of those who worshiped there before the war. The little village is in a generally thriving condition, and bids fair to reestablish its long-held reputation as an attractive seaside resort, as many of the friends and guests of the Normal School have already found it a pleasant place of retreat from bitter northern storms, with its unsurpassed beauty of situation, and its climate, temperate in the main (though not entirely free from the terrors of the frost), the pleasures of midwinter boating on its land-locked waters, its Christmas roses, and its *perennial* oysters. It is the center of historic ground, and is surrounded by places well worth visiting, whose names recall associations of thrilling interest: Yorktown, Newport News, Norfolk, Big Bethel, are all within a radius of twenty miles. Two miles down the creek, at the mouth of Hampton Roads, is Fortress Monroe, interesting both in its historic past and its present busy life as a military post and artillery school, under command of Major-General W. F. Barry. Nearer still is another friendly neighbor of the school, the Chesapeake Military Asylum, as it is popularly called, the Southern branch of the National Home for Disabled Volunteers. The large, commanding edifice occupied before the war by one of the principal young ladies' seminaries of Virginia now shelters nearly four hundred invalid veterans, under the kind and able command of Captain Woodfin, U. S. Volunteers, and is a monument of the nation's gratitude, at all times worthy of inspection.

These are some of the attractions of Hampton, but among them the school itself surely ranks first, in view of what it has done and is doing to solve some of the grave problems left to the country by the decisions of the war, the problems of reconstruction for blacks and whites, of the readjustment of disturbed social equilibriums, of what to do with the negro, and what to do for the South.

The influence of a live, active power like this institution should certainly be felt in the circle immediately surrounding it, and may claim some place among the causes of Hampton's growth. Not only by adding somewhat to the business of the place, but by making itself and its objects respected, by giving honor to industry, and working out the visible results of skilled labor and practical education, by manifesting a spirit of helpful sympathy and honest intent to the community around it, it has established a position therein which is cordially acknowledged, and deserves such estimate by the thinking men of the South as was expressed on the last commencement-day by Rev. Dr. Ruffner:

"It would have been easy to establish a school here that would have been hateful to the intelligent people of the State, and been mischievous just in proportion to its success. But this school is worthy of all praise. Its aim has been honest and single. It is just what it seems to be--a purely educational institution, giving satisfaction to all and offense to none."

Such, up to this time, has been the history of the "Hampton Normal and Agricultural Institute," and the noteworthy fact stands out, we trust, clearly enough that the school is a *growth*; no unfinished, one-sided, unstable creation of an individual whim, but a natural, healthy growth. It has not been forced upon the people; it is not a makeshift until something better can be had; it has not been endowed by any one person, to be at the mercy of a changing humor; but, on the contrary, it has met a people's imperative demand, and having met that demand honestly, it bears within itself the reason for its permanent continuance and increase, while the fact that its acres have been bought and its bricks laid with money from a thousand different sources has rooted its claims in a multitude of hearts, and made its future very hopeful.

The system adopted in the first instance by the officers and trustees has been, with some modifications, continued, and has certain peculiarities which entitle it to such a description as can best be given from the personal observation of one who, as a teacher, has obtained a familiar knowledge of its working and its results. The following pages are therefore devoted to an account of the actual condition of the school, giving, also, something of the experience of the troupe of colored singers known as the "Hampton Students," who were sent out in the winter of '72-3, in the hope that the appeal of their music and their faces might enable the Hampton treasury to meet the calls made upon it by the rapidly increasing student-roll. The endeavor has been, in presenting this brief history to the public, to create, if possible, an intelligent and lasting interest in the future of Hampton, and to show that, while its work was at the outset necessarily experimental, the school has already become theoretically and practically a success, needing only a reasonable increase of means in order to take its place as one of the most important institutions of the South.

A TEACHER'S WITNESS.

BY M. F. A.

IT is evident that the only test of any system of education which can be of value is the test of practical application, and when the founders of the Hampton Normal and Agricultural Institute were called upon to decide as to the general character of the school they were about to establish, they were keenly alive to the importance of making use of all possible means to insure the success of their unique undertaking, an undertaking which was at that time so far without precedent as to be to many minds simply chimerical.

First of all, therefore, they consulted the needs of those who were destined to become the pupils of the school, and then took careful account of the experience of various experimentalists, a course which resulted in the adoption of a "Manual Labor System," which, by right of the originality of certain of its features, may fairly be known as the "Hampton System." This system, as it stands, is remarkable; because, while it has drawn largely from different sources in our own and other countries, its application to a people scarcely emerged from, slavery made requisite certain peculiarities which are particularly worthy of notice as being a direct result of an unparalleled social revolution.

The slaves, whose emancipation made such a school as Hampton possible, found, as the inevitable effect of their enslavement, their chief misfortune in deficiency of character rather than in ignorance. They were improvident, without self-reliance, and immoral. On the other hand, they possessed the virtues of patience and cheerfulness, a hearty desire for improvement, especially in book knowledge, while in many cases there existed a religious fervor often amounting to a form of superstition, so vivid was, and still is, their belief in all conditions of the supernatural, from God to Satan. Four millions of these slaves were set free with absolutely no preparation for a state of which the novelty alone was sufficient to blind or dazzle their unused faculties, and with scarcely more than nominal restraint or assistance, were left to shift for themselves, in the midst of the ruins of the only social law of which they had any experience.

It can hardly be necessary to allude in other than the briefest terms to the condition of the Southern States directly after the war; and, indeed, there are only two facts which require just here to be dwelt upon--namely, first, that the slaveholders bereft of their slaves were almost as helpless as the slaves, so far as concerned the retrieval of their fortunes; for not only had six generations of slave-owning in a marked manner enfeebled the power of a majority of the dominant race, but the annihilation of property in men left the South in almost universal bankruptcy; second, that enforced labor being no longer to be had, the future of the South depended upon the speedy creation of a class of skilled and willing laborers, and that such laborers were to be found mainly in the vast army of unemployed freed men and women.

No one for whom the question had any interest could fail to see that the best hope of both whites and blacks lay in a wise training of both races for the work that was waiting for them, and the establishment in the South of schools that should afford such training. General Armstrong, stationed as an officer of the Freedmen's Bureau at Hampton, where the work had been already so well begun by the American Missionary Association, saw the importance of locating one of these schools at that point, central as it was to the great negro population of Virginia, North Carolina, and Maryland, a population numbering more than a million. The seed sown years ago in far-off Pacific islands sprang now into quick fruitage, for a youth passed among a people similar in many respects to the Anglo-African, gave him a peculiar power to grasp the problem of the successful establishment of a normal school for freedmen. The intelligent and liberal support of the American Missionary Association and the Freedman's Bureau enabled him, when appointed Principal of the Hampton Institute, to adopt a manual-labor system, his opinion being that such a system, carefully prepared, would best meet the exigencies of the case. He had seen the successful working of such schools among the semi-civilized natives of the Sandwich Islands, and his own views were strengthened by the testimony of some of the oldest of the pioneer missionaries, one of whom, the Rev. Dwight, Baldwin, D.D., in writing to Hampton, gives briefly the result of their experiments among the Hawaiian people. He says, "The Lahainaluna school has been a great light in the midst of the Hawaiian Islands. For the whole forty years that it has been in operation, it has been a mighty power to aid us in enlightening and Christianizing the Hawaiian race. Without this seminary, how could we have furnished anything like efficient teachers for a universal system of common schools, a system which has already made almost the entire people of these islands readers of the Bible? Then, also, of all the native preachers and pastors who have been enlisted in this good work, it has been very rare to find one particularly useful who has not been previously trained in this seminary. And throughout the islands, except just about the capital, where foreigners are employed, the execution of the laws depends entirely upon educated Hawaiians. It has always been a manual-labor school. This arose partly from necessity; but a second reason was that all our plans for elevating this people were laid from the beginning to give them not only learning, but also intelligent appreciation of their duties as men and citizens, and to prepare them in every way for a higher civilization. The plan pursued here in this respect is the same, I believe, essentially, as you have pursued at the Hampton Institute. It is the plan dictated by nature and reason, and if you pursue it thoroughly and wisely, it will make your Institute a speedy blessing to all the freedmen of the South."

From such witnesses as these, and from the carefully reported experience of schools in Germany, France, and Great Britain, all possible facts were obtained, and Hampton, in 1868, was inaugurated as a manual-labor school. To the completeness with which it has fulfilled its original design, many witnesses have borne testimony, and that one given by the Rev. George L. Chancy, of Boston, in January, 1870, is especially interesting from its impartiality:

"This school, open alike to men and women of every race, but only attended now by freedmen, sets the rule of education to the whole nation. The State which is kept standing on the threshold of our Union carries in her hands the ideal school. The Northern men and women who went South to teach have learned more than they have taught. Driven by the necessity of their impoverished pupils, they have learned to combine an education of the hand with the education of the mind. It is already written in the proof-sheets of the new history, that Massachusetts learned from Virginia how to keep school."

At the very outset, the trustees were wise enough to reject the theory that the manual labor performed by students must necessarily be made profitable, but based their efforts upon the fact that their system had for its primary object the education of the pupils. They devoted themselves to obtaining for the scholars such advantages as the nature of their past lives made specially desirable; and realizing distinctly that true manhood is the ultimate end of education, of experience, and of life, they grounded their work on the conviction that the best and most practical training is that of the faculties which should guide and direct all the others. They appreciated also the comparative uselessness of educating the men of any race when their mothers and sisters are left untrained, and resolved that the Hampton system should include both sexes under the most favorable possible circumstances.

The school opened in April, 1868, with twenty (20) scholars and two (2) academic teachers, while for the term beginning September, 1873, the catalogue shows us a roll of twelve (12) teachers in the academic department, six (6) teachers in the industrial departments, and two hundred and twenty-six (226) pupils. These figures in themselves represent success, and the reports of the various departments furnish still further proof that the division of labor and study has been satisfactory to teachers and scholars, while the pecuniary result is altogether better than was originally expected. At the opening of the present term, the system may be considered as matured, and the division of the school into academic and industrial departments, each with its separate corps of teachers, under the control of one principal, has been found to afford the required advantages.

CHAPEL AND FARM MANAGER'S HOUSE.

The farm of one hundred and ninety (190) acres, which includes seventy-two (72) acres of the "Segar Farm," recently purchased with the avails of the Land Scrip Fund, is managed by an experienced farmer; and for the purpose of interfering as little as possible with recitations, the students are divided into five squads, which are successively assigned one day in each week for labor on the farm. All the boys also work a half or the whole of every Saturday, during the term. Each student has therefore, each week, from a day and a half to two days of labor on the farm, for which he is allowed from five to ten cents an hour, or from seventy-five cents to two dollars a week, according to his ability.

From two to four hired men are steadily employed to take care of teams, drive market-wagon, etc.; but the greater part of the farm-work is done by the young men of the school. Market-gardening is carried on extensively, hundreds of dollars' worth of asparagus, cabbages, white and sweet potatoes, peas, and peaches being annually sold at Fortress Monroe, or shipped to the markets of Baltimore, Philadelphia, New-York, and Boston. Between twenty and thirty gallons of milk are daily supplied to the boarding department of the school or sold in the neighborhood, at an average price of thirty cents per gallon.

LION AND JOHN SOLOMON.

The introduction of blooded stock, a French Canadian stallion, Ayrshire cattle, Chester, pigs, etc., is directly benefiting the farmers of the surrounding country, the appreciation of the value of these importations being shown by the fact that at the Virginia and North-Carolina State Agricultural Fair held in Norfolk, in the autumn of 1872, three first prizes were taken by normal-school stock.

The division of the one hundred and forty-six (146) acres under cultivation during the past year is as follows:

- Corn . . . . . 55 acres.
- Wheat . . . . . 35 acres.
- Barley . . . . . 4 acres.

- Corn-fodder . . . . . 6 acres.
- Peas . . . . . 4 acres.
- Early potatoes . . . . . 7 acres.
- Sweet potatoes . . . . . 4 acres.
- Asparagus . . . . . 3 1/2 acres.
- Cabbages . . . . . 1 acre.
- Turnips, carrots, etc. . . . . . 3 acres.
- Snap beans . . . . . 2 acres.
- Oats sowed with clover . . . . . 8 acres.
- Garden vegetables . . . . . 2 1/2 acres.
- Broomcorn . . . . . 1/2 acre.
- Strawberries . . . . . 1/2 acre.
- Peach orchard (800 trees) . . . . . 6 acres.
- Pear orchard and nursery . . . . . 2 acres.
- Cherry and plum orchard . . . . . 2 acres.
- Apple orchard . . . . . 4 acres.

THE PRINTING-OFFICE.

THE PRINTING-OFFICE.

    The printing-office connected with the school was founded by the gift of one thousand dollars from Mrs. Augustus Hemenway, of Boston, and was opened for business November 1st, 1871, beginning with two small presses, a second-hand Washington hand-press, and a quarter-medium Gordon press, to which was added last winter, by the liberality of Messrs. Richard Hoe & Co., of New-York, a first-class hand stop cylinder press, a gift of very great value to the school. About the same time, a donation of nearly three hundred dollars' worth of new type was made by Messrs. Farmer, Little & Co., New York. These generous gifts have greatly increased the working facilities of the office, which is the only one in Hampton. By the job-work which it is thus able to take in, it is established upon a paying basis, as well as enabled to offer greater advantages of work to the students. The boys employed in the office are selected as showing particular aptitude for the business, and the majority of them make rapid progress--one indeed having been able during the past year to pay his way in school by work done out of school hours.

The first cost of the office and its furniture was paid by friends in the North, and the neighborhood affords a fair regular supply of job-work, while an illustrated paper, *The Southern Workman*, is published monthly, for circulation among the industrial classes of the South, among whom it has met with a very favorable reception.[*] *See Note 3 in Appendix.

In addition to their training on the farm and in the printing office, the male students are employed in the carpenter and blacksmith-shops, shoe-shop and paint-shop, where most of the ordinary repairs and light work of the establishment are done. These different departments of manual labor furnish such variety of instruction as admirably prepares the students for the uncertainty of their future lives, and enables them at the end of the three years' course to choose between several occupations, in any one of which they can serve with honor and profit to themselves.

GIRLS' INDUSTRIAL ROOM.

The young women of the school are also provided with an Industrial Department (founded by a Northern lady), where they are taught to cut and fit garments, and to use various sewing-machines, the articles which they produce being sold to members of the school or to persons in the neighborhood; and the report of the founder of this department is, that "the young women employed are in most cases faithful and industrious, eager and grateful for the opportunity of earning something toward their expenses, while their spirit and conduct in connection with the department have, except in a few cases, been good in all respects." In addition to the special work of this department, the girls are taught the ordinary duties of a household, laundry-work, etc., and are thus fitted to become cleanly and thrifty housekeepers, while their personal habits are carefully superintended, and they are constantly instructed in the simpler laws of health.

The labor performed by the students during the last two years and its results are so essential a part of the school's history, that the following extract from the Treasurer's report is given, as embodying statistics of real value:

SESSION OF 1871-2.

- Students on labor list 95

CREDITS FOR LABOR.

- On farm $1,360 01
- Boarding Department (house-work) 1,087 35
- Girls' Industrial Department (sewing, etc.) 625 03
- School-work (accountants, janitors, carpenters, etc.) 826 01
- Shoemakers 74 95
- Printing-office 280 62

Total $4,253 97

SESSION OF 1872-3.

- Students on labor list 170

CREDITS FOR LABOR.

- On farm $1,873 93
- Boarding Department (house-work) 1,408 90
- Girls' Industrial Department (sewing) 701 08
- Printing-office 239 91
- School-work (accountants, janitors, carpenters, etc.) 1,018 62
- Shoemakers 86 37
- Work on buildings 53 26

Total $5,382 07

Hampton and Its Students

The rates of credit for labor are adjusted according to its market value, and the training which the students receive in the thorough examination and understanding of their accounts, which are made out in detail monthly by the Treasurer, is of permanent and incalculable benefit to them.

One of the fundamental principles of the school is that nothing should be given which can be earned or in any way supplied by the pupil, and in consonance with this principle, regular personal expenses for board, etc., rated at $10 a month, are thrown upon each student, to be paid by them, half in cash and half in labor. Good mechanics, first-rate farm-hands and seamstresses can earn the whole of this amount, but those pupils whose labor is of little value, and who are destitute, being either orphaned or with impoverished parents, require and receive proper aid, nearly one third of the boarders having been assisted by direct donations during the past term. To this purpose are devoted the annual income from the "Peabody Fund" of $800, and such part of the cash receipts of the school as may be found necessary; personal relief being made systematically exceptional and closely contingent upon high merit.

Among the most prominent dispensers of such aid are Mr. and Mrs. George Dixon, of the English Society of Friends, and during six years teachers among the freedmen in the South, at their own charges. They are now giving personal aid to forty-five of their former pupils as members of this institution. To this end, they have secured funds by personal effort in England. Mr. Dixon was for twenty-five years head of the Agricultural College at Great Ayton, Yorkshire, England, and now, as a resident on the Normal School premises, and lecturer on Agricultural Chemistry, adds very materially to the resources of the faculty.

While everything is thus done to cultivate a spirit of self-reliance and independence, it has been proved, as a matter of fact, that beyond this payment of actual personal expenses, the colored youth of the South are not able to go. These young men and women at Hampton strain every nerve to meet the daily cost of their food and clothing, and it is beyond a doubt that if they are to get any education at all, such education must be *given* to them. Instruction, therefore, is the central point of our work, and entails the chief outlay, to meet which, the actual cost of educating each individual, estimated at $70 per annum, has to be secured by voluntary contributions. In order, therefore, to keep up that practical, personal interest in the school which, so long as it depends upon private charity, is of the first importance, a system of scholarships has been instituted and found to be most successful.

These scholarships are divided as follows: Annual scholarships of $70, scholarships for the course of three years of $210, and permanent scholarships of $1000, the interest

Hampton and Its Students

of which is forever devoted to the education of a pupil. Last year, 152 annual (or $70) scholarships were contributed, many of the donors of which have signified their intention to renew them, thus meeting the heaviest present expense of the school; but the desire of the trustees is to establish, as rapidly as possible, permanent (or $1000) scholarships, and a number of professorships, of from $10,000 to $25,000 each, which will save the time and cost of annual collections, and insure the future of the institution.

The Rev. Thomas K. Fessenden, of Farmington, Ct., over two years ago undertook the work of securing an endowment. His efforts have been successful beyond expectation (see note in Treasurer's report in Appendix); and in this connection, it is not out of place to mention that Mr. Fessenden is the founder of the Girls' Industrial School at Middletown, one of the noblest charities in Connecticut. As a member of the Legislature of that State, his influence secured the passage of a satisfactory law in behalf of that school, and his personal solicitations resulted in an endowment of nearly $100,000 for it.

The wholesome and pleasant relation which grows up between the givers of our scholarships and their recipients, does in no way abate the self-respect of the latter, and entails no loss of stimulus to hard work; for, in the words of the Principal of the school, "it is helping those who help themselves, and, as results show, is productive of sound scholarship and Christian manliness." Each student who is thus assisted is expected, in the first instance, to write a letter of acknowledgment to the unknown friend whose interest is so substantially shown, and the donor not seldom finds an unexpected source of happiness in the quaint expressions of gratitude which reach him in the name of some dark-faced boy or girl hungry for books and their mysterious contents.

The three classes of the school--Seniors, Middlers, and Juniors-- are carefully divided according to the ability of their members, and the standard of scholarship is unvarying, no individual being retained unless there is shown both desire and power to keep up with the class studies, although so much hearty assistance is given by the teachers, both in and out of school hours, that only the hopelessly stupid or careless need fear expulsion. The teacher who in her turn takes charge of the boys' or girls' evening study hour finds her office no sinecure, as she moves among the desks, stopping here and there to answer the impatient appeal of lifted hands with the few words of advice or encouragement that shall make the crooked ways straight through the intricacies of algebra, or the labyrinth of moods and tenses.

THE ASSEMBLY-ROOM.

As to the ability of these colored students in comparison with whites, the verdict of the teachers is unanimous; the average in the Hampton classes, they agree, differs little from the average in any ordinary Northern school, while the marked eagerness to learn compensates, to a great extent, for the entire lack of culture in past generations and of home-training in the present. To meet this want, which is one of the most serious hindrances in the colored student's road to learning, efforts are made to give them as much general information as possible outside of the regular line of school study, by familiar lectures upon topics, of common interest. These are always listened to with eager interest, especially when made graphic by personal experience, or enlivened by blackboard illustrations. A daily bulletin of news made up from the leading journals, and published on a large blackboard in the main hall, is found another great help in rousing these wakening minds to a sense of what is going on in the world around them.

I have never seen, I can scarcely imagine a more hopeful picture than is offered by some of the more advanced students of our school, for there is a quick gratitude for every word of explanation which helps them on their difficult path, to which no heart can fail to respond, while the absolute famine for knowledge which distinguishes them from ordinary students finds its answer in the brain of every true teacher. No one can live among these people, much less can attempt to open for them the way into the wondrous kingdoms of Nature and Art, without gaining in return new views of the possibilities of humanity, and strong faith that the future of this long-enduring race will yet redeem its past.

Without fanaticism, and without special prejudice in favor of the negroes, the teachers at Hampton, going down from Northern schools and Northern homes, are fair witnesses as to the capacities and characters of their pupils, and I am only their representative in saying that to educate these ex-slaves pays in every sense.

The ex-slaveholders in Virginia, and generally in the other Southern States, comprehend the necessity of negro education, and are willing, not only to put no obstacles in the way of schools already established, but to assist them wherever possible, as in Virginia, where one third of the land scrip of the State was last year voted to Hampton, and, where the head of the Department of Education, Rev. W. H. Ruffner, D.D.,* *See Appendix, Note 4.
has been one of Hampton's best friends, showing an earnest desire to second the action of the school officials with the prestige which his position gives. The better class of Southerners appreciate, of course, that the economic value of an educated negro is far greater than that of an uneducated one, and their desire to develop the resources of their country would alone lead them to see that on this point the interests of the white and the colored population coincide; but aside from this, there is a growing sense of the justice of including the negro in any future scheme of popular education, which will prove a valuable auxiliary to the conviction of the expediency of such a course. As a result of this, the State governments are gradually assuming the charge of the elementary instruction of the colored people, but the feeling against mixed schools is still so strong that they are shut out from all Southern collegiate institutions, and consequently are able to get no professional training except in schools established, like Hampton, especially for them.

Hampton and Its Students

As has been before noticed, the experience of the most successful missionaries, all the world over, as well as that of the leading practical educators of the South, induces them to prefer always trained teachers of the same race as those whom they are destined to teach, and already the demand for colored teachers in Virginia alone could not be supplied by all the Southern States together. To-day, thousands of colored children in Virginia and the Carolinas are without elementary schools, not from any unwillingness on the part of the State governments to supply them, not because salaries and school-houses are wanting, but solely because there are no teachers; and it would hardly be possible to find more speedy means for facilitating popular education in the South than the establishment of institutions devoted primarily to the training of colored teachers. Hampton is doing just this work, or nine tenths of the graduates she sends out become at once teachers of colored schools, and testimony to the thoroughness of the training they have received pours in upon us from Virginia school-officers--all of them ex-slaveholders and ex-officers of the Confederate army-- who, without exception, report more than favorably as to the ability and conduct of the teachers supplied by Hampton.[*]

[*] See Appendix, Note 5.

In the growth of such an institution as this, in the midst of so disturbed a society as still exists in the South, there must arise, now and again (in spite of the determined efforts of its officers to prevent political complications), questions involving the rights and duties of the colored people as citizens and responsible political agents, and the chief danger of the race lies only too evidently in the plasticity and ignorance which put them completely under the control of any superficial or unprincipled men whose ambition may point in the direction of party leadership. This blind leading of the blind is already producing its result in the spread of the belief that political rights are better to be obtained by self-assertion and selfish struggle, than by studying to acquire such fitness for power, that power cannot be withheld, and this false doctrine can only be counteracted by the introduction of intelligent political opinion among the more advanced class of colored people. Nowhere can such opinions be more quickly and widely disseminated than from a school which strives to be a center of

READING-ROOM.

moral as well as intellectual light; and while at Hampton there is constant endeavor to inculcate an honest appreciation of the importance of political duties, the young men who graduate from there are earnestly encouraged to value principle far above individual aggrandizement. There can be no doubt that the white leaders of both parties in the South have made shameful use of the ignorance of their negro fellow-citizens, and the only weapons with which such duplicity and dishonor can be successfully fought are those which education furnishes. Any institution having such work before it must, from the outset, be independent of State control, and while State aid under certain restrictions should be a matter of course, yet the school system should be entirely untrammeled by the chains of this or that political party. In this respect, Hampton is most fortunately free,

Hampton and Its Students

having steered between Scylla and Charybdis to take finally an independent stand which commands respect from all parties.

The service which Hampton, in a political aspect, is doing for the State is rapidly obtaining the acknowledgment it merits; for to withstand dangers arising from ignorant combination is just now (in the absence of social criticism and intelligent public opinion) one of the problems most urgently pressing on Southern society, and those most interested recognize already that no effective legislation can be looked for in the face of the dense ignorance existing among the poorer classes of the South, especially when such ignorance is manipulated by adroit and conscienceless leaders. No radical change in the political condition can be expected except as the mass of the people are gradually led up to a higher plane of thought; and the speediest means of effecting this advancement is found in schools whose students, going out in their turn as teachers, influence the life of a whole neighborhood, and being of one blood with those among whom they labor, know their needs, and can rouse and purify them by the force of personal example. The value of the Hampton school in this respect is neither imaginary nor sentimental, but altogether practical and susceptible of direct proof, and the acknowledgment of this comes to us constantly from the most satisfactory source, namely, from educated Southern men themselves, who watch the progress of our educational experiment with exceeding interest, and often are ready with kindly words of appreciation, which in their mouths are full of meaning. Undoubtedly, the natural, though rapid development of the plan of the Hampton trustees has had much to do with its acceptance by Southerners of every shade of political sentiment; for its growth from very humble beginnings has been so completely in accordance with the law of demand and supply, that the most determined prejudices have faded away before its steady progress; and to-day those Southerners who know anything of its work give it the foremost rank among the educational institutions south of Washington.

As an economic experiment, the manual-labor System, as applied at Hampton, is an undoubted success[*]--that is, the expenses of the school are reduced to a minimum, while the students, not overburdened with physical labor, come to their books with fresh interest and untired faculties, and not only lose none of the advantages of their three years' intellectual culture, but, on the other hand, gain much by the varied training in the practical duties of life, which opens to them new fields of labor, and offers fresh stimulants to honest ambition. It is no more than true to say, that in this respect Hampton has exceeded the hopes of its founders, having demonstrated that the properly systematized manual labor of both male and female students can, in this country, be made a sure source of revenue to the school, without in any degree lessening the ability of such students to receive intellectual culture.

Hampton and Its Students

* See Appendix, Note 6.

But while Hampton has a wide sphere of usefulness in its relation to the State, and as an educational experiment upon the largest scale is of interest to all lovers of humanity, it is as a noble and beautiful charity that it makes its highest claim upon us; and in this view, it is difficult to speak of it in terms that will not seem to be the result of an exaggerated sympathy. At the risk of such accusation, a close acquaintance with the daily life of the school and a personal intimacy with its teachers and students induce me to offer what I believe to be the experience not of one teacher only, but of the whole working corps of the school, in regard to the efficiency of the academic department and the general characteristics of its pupils. During the term of 1873-4, the number of students enrolled was 226, who for the academic course were divided among twelve teachers, most of them trained graduates of the best Northern schools. The plan of the school subdivides these three classes into smaller sections of from twenty to fifty scholars, according to the nature of the study,*

* See Appendix, Note 7.

and these are passed from one recitation to another during the school hours, which are from nine till three, with proper intervals for dinner and recess. The training which they receive is, I believe, more thorough than that given in most schools, because, by reason of the ignorance of the students on all general as well as special subjects, it is necessary to begin at the foundation and to reiterate instruction until permanent impressions are produced, while, the number of studies being limited, the teachers are able to do justice to the branches which they undertake.

There are doubtless schools for colored people in the South whose list of studies is much longer and more pretentious than that of Hampton, but as the point to be considered is not so much what the negro at high pressure is capable of learning, as what for his own present good he most needs to learn, a course which includes merely the ordinary English branches, while surrounding the student with influences calculated to mould his character and elevate his whole nature, is far more desirable than one which promises to turn out graduates proficient in a dead language or facile in oratory.

More important than quickness in thought or correctness in speech, are the fundamental habits of a life, and this fact holds its proper place in our students' training. Every day, the young men are drilled, without arms, in various evolutions, to acquire promptness in obedience and in action, and a good carriage. They are closely inspected from head to foot every day, and want of neatness in attire is a matter for discipline.

Hampton and Its Students

Quarters also are subject to daily inspection, and penalties are sure for any want of order. Standing in the school depends quite as much upon faithfulness in labor as upon proficiency in study. Rank is determined, as nearly as possible, by character and real value, and not by recitation-marks.

The programme of work at Hampton is simple enough at first sight, but it must be remembered that the minds for which it is laid down are absolutely fresh and untutored, while only too curious in the pursuit of knowledge.

There are scholars and scholars, and it is impossible to describe the difference between a class in Hampton and a class of the same relative age and intelligence in a Northern school. It would be good indeed if I could put down upon paper the enthusiasm, the quick answers of tongue and eye, the honest perseverance, the wild guessing, the half-incredulous astonishment with which some bit of history, some scientific experiment, or mayhap some ringing poem or well-demonstrated problem, is received by a group of dusky scholars, as they stand gathered about the teacher, who for them is an oracle, a heaven-sent messenger. Such eagerness and earnestness of purpose make study what it should be, a delight to teacher and pupil, and fatigue and dullness are unknown conditions in the midst of scholars to whom the smallest fact is a treasure, and in whom every day shows change and growth.

I can scarcely ask those who are strangers to such work to believe how rapidly these young men and women develop under the novel influences brought to bear upon them by teachers thoroughly interested in their progress, nor how quickly they grasp all that marks their inferiority to the Anglo-Saxons with whom they are associating. When placed in contact with cultivated white teachers, our colored students are not long in realizing how great is the height which they must scale in order to win a true equality, and their appreciation of the value of education and opportunity is so keen as to seem at times almost superstitious. Yet this rarely discourages them, and their characteristic as students is a determination to sacrifice much, and labor to their utmost for the education which to them is the password to the good things of this world. They are by no means slow in the acquirement of knowledge; indeed, when one considers through how many generations the intellectual faculties of the race have lain dormant, it is astonishing that the mental peculiarities and weaknesses of this first generation of freedmen are not more marked and difficult to overcome than they are practically found to be.

Our students learn with average readiness, and show more than average perseverance, but find their chief obstacle in an inability to assimilate the ideas which they receive, an obstacle largely to be accounted for by the fact that they have had little previous education, and as children formed no fixed habits of thought. The formulation of ideas and their expression in words are invariably difficult for them, and at times, it is fairly pitiful to watch their efforts to catch and crystallize into language a thought which they feel to be slipping from them back into the realms of mystery whence it came. But, in the main, our verdict as teachers is that they are already good students, and bid fair to become better, while the difference in the youth who enters Hampton and the youth who leaves it at the end of a three years' course is so great as to be the only personal argument required among those who know the school in favor of every possible increase of its power and facilities.

Last year, we had the sorrow of turning away from our doors many an applicant whose only hope lay with us, because our buildings were already more than full; and all through the chill

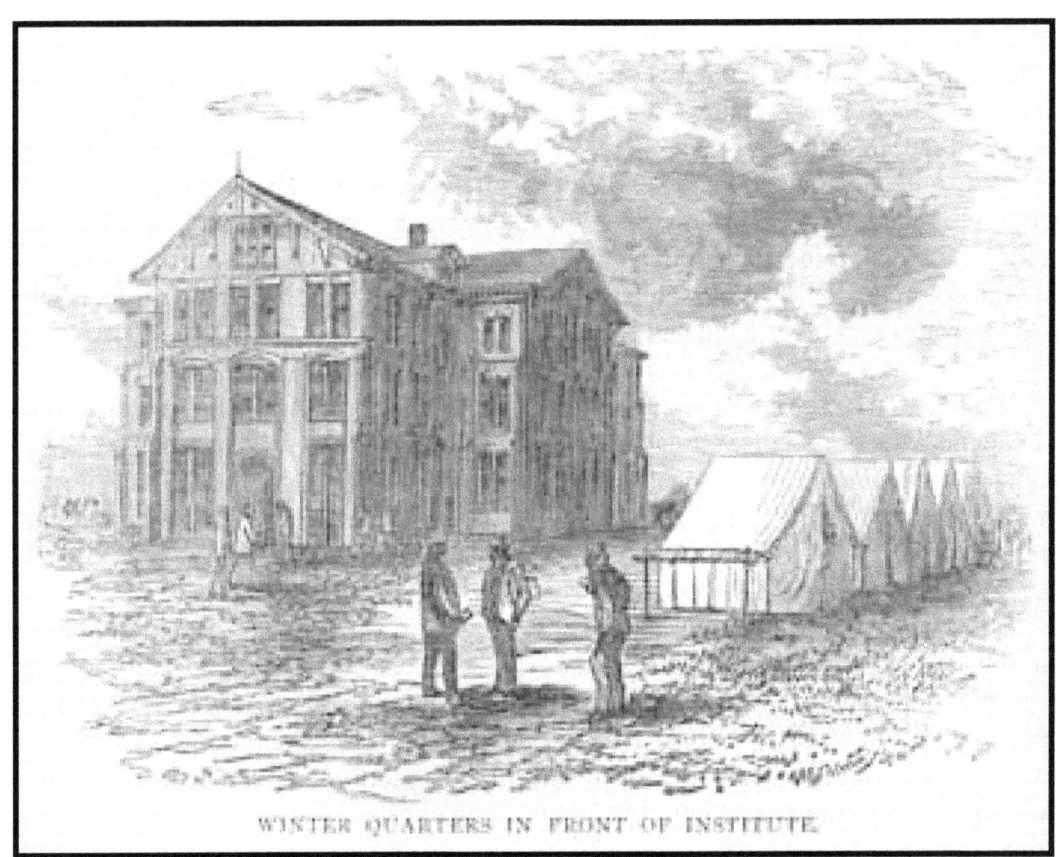

WINTER QUARTERS IN FRONT OF INSTITUTE.

Virginian winter, our boys, in squads of twenty-four to thirty at a time, are lodged in tents whose canvas walls are frail protection against the stormy winds which sometimes visit that open sea-coast. I have looked from my window, on many a frosty night, at those icicle-fringed tents, and through many a wild morning have watched the heavy Southern rain beating upon their gray roofs, wishing in my heart that those in North or South who tell us that "negro" is but a synonym for laziness and cowardice could see for themselves the testimony borne by that little settlement of tents standing unsheltered within a stone's throw of the sea. There is as much downright pluck under these black skins as under any white ones, and the admirable courage and ambition of the freed people deserve substantial recognition and encouragement; for, however heavy is the tax laid upon them, they have shown themselves ready to meet it, for the sake of the much-coveted prize of education.

We who, in God's providence, were appointed to bring to these children of His their wearily-looked-for freedom, are to-day, in His sight, responsible in great part for the use they make of it; and to have broken their chains only to leave them in an ignorance worse than slavery would truly be a deed unworthy of our country and our Christianity. We have set them free, and now we have before us the plain duty of teaching them to use their freedom, and to that end there seems little doubt such schools as Hampton are the swiftest means. Indeed, there is no other way than this; and Hampton, already securely founded, has every claim upon the attention and generosity of the public, to whom we appeal, in the name of a benighted race, for the speedy aid which shall lift from the colored people of the South the burden of past misfortune, and save their white brothers from years of struggle and social disorder.

We want more room, we want money to put up new buildings which shall receive and welcome the crowd of waiting students for whom with our present means we can do nothing, and the bulk of this money must come from the North, for the South is no longer able even to support those institutions that are dearest to its national honor, and the State has for the present done its utmost for Hampton.

In asking for an endowment for our school, we draw attention especially to the fact that in these days the centralization of resources for advanced education is all-important. "Scatter your resources for primary education; concentrate your resources for advanced education," has become an axiom; and one such institution as Hampton, fully endowed and thoroughly furnished with the machinery of education, can do ten times the work of two or three institutions indifferently equipped and constantly struggling for existence. In this country, where the population is spread over so wide an area, these educational foci, to which the youth of the land are drawn by the attraction of advantages to be obtained nowhere else, are far more economical of public resources than any system of scattered colleges, which only impoverish each other and the State, while the experience of nations older than our own demonstrates the great increase of intellectual power to be obtained by the plan of concentration. Hampton's field practically embraces the States of Virginia and North Carolina, including a colored population of nearly a million souls, while it has always on its student-roll, representatives from several other States.

Atlanta University, Atlanta, Ga., Fisk University, at Nashville, Tenn., and Howard University, at Washington, D. C., all have similar relation to the two or three States around them, and the radius of their influence has, in each case, a sweep of hundreds of miles, though, as a matter of course, there is no practical interference. There are many minor and very meritorious institutions devoted to the freedmen, chiefly denominational, but competition for students is not likely to arise in this generation, and there is noticeably more tendency to concentration in the South than in the North.

Hampton, a school which sprang into life in answer to the cry of a people hungry for knowledge, needs, in round numbers, an endowment of $300,000, besides its building fund, to make it what it should be, an institution of the highest order, amply supplied with means to carry on the work which it has begun. New buildings are needed at once, especially for the young women, who are not able to bear the hardships which the young men willingly undergo, and the walls of "Virginia Hall," inclosing chapel, dining-room, and dormitories, have risen, brick by brick, as the money has come to us from kindly Northern friends, who believe, as we do, that their gifts are made to serve a noble end. This "Hall" will cost, unfurnished, $75,000, and will in itself be an education for our students, for here, they will find those appliances of civilization which, while they are to us every-day matters, are to them an important part of a new life. Here they will be taught the cleanliness, order, and decencies of manner which are as necessary in any scheme of education for the negro as the spelling-book and the pen, and here they will be made gradually but surely to feel the influence of that careful physical, training to which most of them are entirely strange.*

A further account of Virginia Hall and its financial history will be found in the chapter devoted to the Hampton student singers.

When this undertaking is complete--and we have faith that that day is not far off--then our young men may claim a like shelter and opportunity, and still must we look chiefly to the North to supply the sinews of war in this fight against ignorance, believing that our prayer, made in the name of a righteous cause, will not go long unanswered.

Writing, as I am permitted to do, as a representative of the teachers of the school, I am able to speak very boldly of its personal aspect, and we who for its sake are not ashamed to beg are of one mind as to the exceeding great reward which this work offers.

BALL CLUB.

The reward to the State is found in the economy of public moneys, and in the protection from that chiefest danger to a democracy, an ignorant population.

The reward to the teacher comes hour by hour in grateful acknowledgment of eye and hand, in the witness of rapid and steady growth toward a better life, in the sure conviction that the result will stand, not for time alone, but for eternity.

And the reward of you who give unto us of that which we have not will come in part in the sight of a noble work going surely on to its accomplishment, but in its completeness only in that hereafter whose blessing is that which passeth understanding.

Hampton and Its Students

In this little volume, we have tried to lay our case fairly before a public to whom it is not altogether unknown, and the facts of Hampton's past history, with the arguments which it has to show in favor of its system, may, we believe, be left to speak for themselves. When we ask, "Shall Hampton be made a permanent, powerful institution?" we think it is evident that the question goes far deeper than its face.

"Shall the four millions of ex-slaves within our national boundaries be educated into useful, honest citizens, or left to corrupt the country and themselves by the strangely fatal power of ignorance?"

"Shall the four millions of God's children thrown helpless upon the nation's charity be lifted up into the equality of Christendom, or left to the dominion of vices from which only a wise and timely care can save them?"

It is, in truth, this that we are asking, and it is to this that you into whose hands heaven has given the means of a people's salvation must give the answer, an answer which, be it remembered, reaches past our feeble questioning, up to the ear of God himself.

THE BUTLER SCHOOL-HOUSE.

THE BUTLER SCHOOL.

    IN the year 1863, when the need of the freed people was most extensive and pressing, General B. F. Butler, being then chief in command at Fortress Monroe, erected with government funds the large wooden building shown in the accompanying cut, which has ever since been known as "The Butler School."

    By the end of that year, above six hundred pupils were gathered within its rough walls, under the care of the Rev. Charles A. Raymond, chaplain of the military post, who conducted it upon the Lancasterian plan--that is, by a system of monitors who, after receiving instruction from the principal, would at once convey it to their pupils. Their task must have been sufficiently perplexing, inasmuch as to the ordinary difficulties of such a school was added the unpleasantness of having all the six hundred children, utterly untrained as they were, huddled into a single room; for in those dark days, the refinements of education were things scarcely to be so much as hoped for. This overcrowding was, however, gradually relieved by the establishment of another school at "Slabtown" (an impromptu suburb of Hampton), and by the building of the "Lincoln School" in 1866, by General Armstrong, with funds supplied by General Howard.

The "Butler" schoolhouse was turned over by the government in 1865 to the American Missionary Association, who supplied it with teachers until it became the property of the trustees of the Hampton Institute, upon whose grounds it stands. In 1871, these trustees requested the public school officers of the county to assume charge of it, reserving the right to nominate its principal. It thus became a free county school, the building, however, remaining the property of the Hampton Institute, whose officers and teachers have kept a watchful eye upon an institution many of whose pupils naturally pass into the more advanced system of Hampton, and graduate from there.

In fact, the school as it now stands is properly preparatory to the "Normal." It is at present under the charge of George and Eunice Dixon, members of the Society of Friends, whose faithful labors for the freedmen, both in this country and in England, have allied them so closely with the Hampton School that they have come finally to take, as teachers, direct interest in its work, and from their present responsible position furnish the following facts in regard to their school:

"It's pupils," writes Mrs. Dixon, "now number 194: 95 girls and 99 boys, running, in age, from five years to twenty-four, and my assistants are a young colored woman, a graduate of the Normal School at Providence, Rhode Island, and a young colored man, a graduate of the Hampton Normal School. There are two divisions--the county school and the preparatory class for the 'Normal;' the latter numbering some forty members, most of whom show a strong desire to learn, and are taught reading, writing, arithmetic, geography, and grammar.

"As this is usually their first experience of school life, we found it, in the beginning, difficult to establish any proper discipline; but the system which we have chosen has been gradually successful, and our school is in comparatively good order. We told our scholars at the outset that there was to be no whipping, but that persistent violation of the rules of the school would result in expulsion, and our resolution has been carried out. One very bad boy has been expelled, with the promise of being allowed to reenter next year if he shows himself deserving of the privilege, and others have been suspended for a day or two, and taken back on a promise of obedience. The plan has worked well, and had a good effect upon the school."

The Superintendent of Public Schools for the county, a Southern gentleman, George M. Peek, Esq., has always shown especial interest in the Butler School, and on

Hampton and Its Students

his last official visit to it expressed his warm gratification with its present condition, which is very encouraging, as its influence among the younger children of the neighborhood is immediate, while its position as preparatory to the higher training of Hampton makes its well-being a matter of serious importance.

M. F. A.

Hampton and Its Students

INTERIOR VIEWS
OF
THE SCHOOL AND THE CABIN.

By

H. W. L.

NEGRO CABIN AT HAMPTON.

INTERIOR VIEWS
OF
THE SCHOOL AND THE CABIN.

A FOUR months' residence in the school, and the occasional opportunities its busy hours afford for researches among the cabins, could scarcely enable one to elaborate any thorough estimate of negro character, or to add anything of value to the discussion of the great question of the freedmen's education, though one quarter of that time is enough to fascinate a novice with the work.

I have to offer instead, therefore, only a few sketches, in simplest light and shade, of the life of bondage and freedom, a few homely interiors of the cabin and school; and the subject is so full of picturesqueness and variety, that I find it difficult to choose from the materials I have collected.

The special interest of most of the portraits is that they are drawn by their own originals. They were obtained from our students by the offer of prizes for the best executed, with the design of private distribution, to interest friends at the North, and for this purpose were left entirely uncorrected and unrevised; and as only the new-comers were asked to write, they are a sample of the material we have to work upon rather than of the results of our work.

After all, this broken speech seems, somehow, on mellow Southern tongues, far more musical than elegant English.

There is a charm of freshness and spontaneity and unconscious eloquence which the first effect of cultivation is often to destroy. A provincial dialect is picturesque as a peasant costume, and can be remodeled only at the expense of its grace.

It is passing rapidly away, and its wearers, naturally perhaps, are eager to cast off and forget as utterly as they may what they regard as a badge of former humiliation, not realizing that they will by and by return and reverently seek for the scattered fragments of a past that was so rich in pathetic, characteristic interest.

There is a present and practical reason for us to collect them that we may more vividly picture to ourselves the necessities of our new fellow-citizens and the duties we still owe to them.

WHAT IS THE PRIVILEGED COLOR?

WE are very frequently asked whether we discover any marked difference in the mental and physical strength of our light and dark students, the prevailing idea seeming to be that the approach to the Anglo-Saxon type must be in all respects an advantage. The school is perhaps as good a field as could be found for the study of this interesting and significant question. We find there all shades of color and various race mixtures, and at first view, the subject seems a puzzling one. The prize biography last year was written by a student who might go from one end of the Union to the other without being suspected of a drop of negro blood; the prize oration, at the laying of the corner stone of Virginia Hall, was delivered by a young man of the most undoubted African type. The question is one, which demands careful and thorough study; and a far more valuable consideration of it than my few months' observation can furnish is the following testimony of General Armstrong:

"The experience of teachers of freedmen, as far as I know, is, that nothing is to be taken for granted, by reason of a light skin.

"There is a good deal in the shape of the head, the facial angle, the general make-up or style of the person, but there are frequent exceptions to this. *Many are better than they look.*

"The light color usually signifies, a less cheery disposition; mulattoes and octoroons often have sad faces, languid eyes, such as are hardly to be found among the pure blacks. In respect to intellect, the latter are quite as apt to be well endowed as the former. The negro is usually more ingenuous and simple than the mixed class.

"The pure-blooded have more endurance than the other, class; they can stand more heat, longer and harder pressure, and seem to have not only more vitality, but to be more likely to last as a people. Infusion of white ideas has proved much more advantageous to the blacks than infusion of white blood.

"There is a good deal of jealousy and caste feeling among the negroes, based on color; a decided preference for being white. This points to the unhappy fact of a lack of pride of race, of esprit de corps as a nation. They seem to have no national idea; and with strong desire and effort for individual improvement, there is little faith in or enthusiasm for themselves as a people with a high destiny.

Hampton and Its Students

"My experience and observation for over two years with the black troops was, that the highest non-commissioned officers were as dark, as a class, as the rest of the regiment. These officers were carefully picked out for their capacity and force, and I took pains to see if they were not of lighter skins than the rest of the rank and file. The best ten in a thousand were about of the average shade. I learned to base no opinion whatever on mere color."

A rather amusing aspect of the question is taken by one of the students who is as white as the whitest of us, and bears the additional peculiarity of red hair in mockery of his undoubted claim to African descent. He sets forth feelingly some of the conflicting advantages and disadvantages of a white skin:

"I am at the Hampton Normal School at present, under the patronage of Mr. George Dixon, for whose goodness to me I shall always feel grateful. On my way to this place, I made the acquaintance of a colored gentleman going to Petersburg, so we journeyed together from Danville, and met with nothing of note till we got to Burkeville, where we had to wait for the cars till next day. On getting off the train, I was immediately beset by porters, who claimed me for their respective hotels. As I could not be well divided, I went with one who promised me a bed for twenty-five cents, (cheap!) As they did not ask my companion to go, I said to him, 'Come, let's go to the hotel.' He and I started, but he was informed by the proprietor that he didn't take colored people at his hotel, and he recommended him to another place; but me they took to the hotel, not knowing that I was colored; so, as they didn't ask, I didn't busy myself telling it, and was comfortably provided for, for the night.

"This was all very well till next day, when, going to get my ticket, I called for a second-class fare, for my money was somewhat short. The agent looked at me with a stare, and said, 'Sir, we only sell second-class tickets to *niggers!* As you are a white man, you must buy a white man's ticket.' Here was a stunner. A colored man made into a white man without his say so ! But I was not to be outdone, and so hunted up my colored friend, who bought me the desired 'nigger's' ticket, and we bid Burkeville farewell."

A WOLF IN SHEEP'S CLOTHING.

IT was a great surprise to me to discover that the element of humor is almost entirely lacking in the character of the Southern negro, though he has a certain sense of the broadly grotesque. He may sometimes furnish material for the humor of others, but it is quite unintentional usually. Whether this be a primitive deficiency or not, I do not know. It may well enough be, owing to the severe schooling of slavery, which left little time for any laughing but that coarser sort which comes from want of thought instead of quickness. Does not this very want, however, itself suggest a means of elevating him--at least a test of his progress? I have always hailed the dawn of a tolerable joke as a promise of light ahead, and I regard the sly, humorous hit at a fleecy official wolf one of the best points in the otherwise well-written sketch which follows:

LORENZO IVY'S LIFE.

"Times have changed so fast in the last ten years, that I often ask myself who am I, and why am I not on my master's plantation, working under an overseer, instead of being here in this institution, under the instruction of a school-teacher. I was born in 1849. My master was very good to his slaves, and they thought a great deal of him. But all of our happy days were over when he went South and caught the cotton fever. He was never satisfied till he moved out there. He sold the house before any of the black people knew anything about it, and that was the beginning of our sorrow. My father belonged to another man, and we knew not how soon we would be carried off from him. Two of my aunts were married, and one of them had ten children, and both of their husbands belonged to another man. Father and my uncles went to their masters and asked them to buy their families. They tried to, but our master wouldn't sell, and told him how many hundred dollars' worth of cotton he could make off us every year, and that we little chaps were just the right size to climb cotton-stalks and pick cotton. But our master and father's master had once agreed that if either one of them ever moved away, he would sell out to the other. So father's master sent for the other gentlemen who heard the conversation, and they said it was true. After a day or two's consideration, he agreed to let him have mother and the seven children for $12,000. That released us from sorrow. But it was not so with my aunts; they had lost all hope of being with their husbands any longer; the time was set for them to start; it was three weeks from the time we were sold. Those three weeks did not seem as long as three days to us who had to shake hands for the last time with those bound together with the bands of love.

"Father said he could never do enough for his master for buying us. They treated us very well for the first three or four years--as the saying was with the black people, they fed us on soft corn at first and then choked us with the husk. When I was large enough to use a hoe, I was put under the overseer to make tobacco-hills. I worked under six overseers, and they all gave me a good name to my master. I only got about three whippings from each of them. The first one was the best; we did not know how good he was till he went away to the war. Then times commenced getting worse with us. I worked many a day without any thing to eat but a tin cup of buttermilk and a little piece of corn bread, and then walk two miles every night or so to carry the overseer his dogs; if we failed to bring them, he would give us a nice flogging.

When the war closed, our master told all the people, if they would stay and get in the crop, he would give them part of it. Most of them left; they said they knew him too well. Father made us all stay, so we all worked on the remainder of the year, just as if Lee hadn't surrendered. I never worked harder in my life, for I thought the more we made, the more we would get. We worked from April till one month to Christmas. We raised a large crop of corn and wheat and tobacco, shucked all the corn and put it in the barn, stripped all the tobacco, and finished one month before Christmas. Then we went to our master for our part he had promised us, but he said he wasn't going to give us anything, and he stopped giving us anything to eat, and said we couldn't live any longer on his land. Father went to an officer of the Freedmen's Bureau, but the officer was like Isaac said to Esau: 'The voice is like Jacob's voice, but the hands are the hands of Esau.' So that was the way with the officer--he had on Uncle Sam's clothes, but he had Uncle Jeff's heart. He said our master said we wasn't worth anything, and he couldn't get anything for us, so father said no more about it.

"We made out to live that winter--I don't know how. In April, 1866, father moved to town where he could work at his trade. He hired all of us boys that were large enough to work in a brickyard for from three to six dollars a month. That was the first time I had tasted the sweet cup of freedom.

"I worked hard all day, and went to night-school two terms and a half, and three months to day-school. When I entered, I could read and spell a little, but did not know one figure from another or any writing. These schools were kept by the Philadelphia Friends' Relief Association, and had very good teachers.

"Father moved next to East Tennessee, and I went to school there three months last winter, and was sent with my sister and two other brothers, by some kind friends who had been my teachers, to this Hampton Normal and Agricultural School.'

HOW AUNT SALLY HUGGED THE OLD FLAG.

A FEW rods from the school-farm gate, on the road to Hampton, stands a row of neat white-washed cabins, curtained by swinging Virginia creepers, and hiding behind mammoth rose-bushes, rosy often till Christmas, though not so last winter, which was the coldest since the war--the war is still the epoch from which all dates are calculated in the South.

On a mild November day, after a vain and unsophisticated search through Hampton for a church, black or white, disposed to keep Thanksgiving, I stopped with a friend at the door that boasts the biggest rosebush, to negotiate for a bouquet to adorn our Thanksgiving dinner table. Aunt Sally's familiar, beaming face and portly form filled the low doorway.

"Come in, come in, chillen. I'se right proud for to see yer. Jes' come in an' sot up to de fiah a bit, whiles I gets ye some posies. We'll hab right smart ob a fros' to-night, *I* believe."

"Thank you, Aunty," we said, accepting her invitation, and stepping into an absurdly tiny bit of a room, neat as waxwork, one side of it entirely taken up by a hugely disproportioned fireplace, a pine "candle-knot" distributing warmth and cheerfulness between the great brass andirons, and a grizzly old "uncle" toasting himself comfortably in the chimney-corner. He rose as we entered, and gave us a minor echo of Aunt Sally's hearty greeting.

"How is it you're all such heathen here in Hampton, Aunty? Not a church-door open on Thanksgiving Day! Got nothing to be thankful for?"

"Laws, yes, dear. I'se been thankful stiddy for de las' ten year--eber since Massa Linkum proclamated dat de black folks was free. But I specs fo' suah you won't find no churches open 'thout it is ober to de Missionary."

"Oh! yes, our chapel is open, and full too, but we thought we'd like to see how you keep the day yourselves."

Well, dear, I neber see it kep' nohow down yere. I reckon it's a kind o' Yankee day, like Christmas is ourn. Dere use to be great doin's ober Christmas in de ol' times."

Hampton and Its Students

"You know you promised to tell us something about those old times someday, Aunty. Have you always lived here, in Hampton?"

"I war raised yere, dear, but our family move ober to Norfolk, an' we war dere when de war took place."

"So you have always belonged to the same family--you had pretty easy times then, hadn't you?"

"Dat's so, dear. I war always employed a-nussin' chillen, you see, an' dey took good keer ob me."

"How many children have you had, Aunty?"

"Fourteen, dear. De las' one war as likely a young gal when she war fifteen as eber you see; tall, an' pretty as a picture', Rosy war--jes' as pretty as a picture'!" and the old face kindled.

"What's become of them all, Aunty?"

"Sold, dear; ebery one on 'em sold down Souf, away from me."

"And Rosy?"

"Sold--to a trader--when she war fifteen; an' jes' as pretty as a picture'. I did hear he sol' her to a man in Richmond, but I neber could fin' nuffin ob her, dough I sent dere sence de war. She's dead--she *must* be."

There was a silence--a convulsion passed across the dark face--one gasp of reviving motherhood shook her great breast, and then her features settled back into their patient repose.

"When de chillen war all done gone," she went on to say, "my missis 'lowed me for to hire my own time, an'I tuk a little cabin jes' out ob Norfolk, an' lived dere by myself eber sence."

"How did you support yourself? Didn't you find it hard work?"

Hampton and Its Students

"I done washin'. I got along well enough tell the war come, an' den it war mighty hard scratchin' for ebery body; but I war too old to be ob much use to 'em, so dey let me stay by myself. I war dere when de Yankees marched into Norfolk."

"That must have been a great time for your people."

"I tell ye what, it war dat. My missis, she tuk fright aforehand, an' move into de country, 'long o' some ob her relations, an' she try for to scare me. 'You'd better come 'long too, Aunty,' she say; 'dem Yankees 'll cotch you. Dey's all got hoofs an' horns like de debil, an' dey won't leave a haar on you' head, fo' suah.' I done tell her what'd dey go to do to an ol' good-for-nuffin nigger like me. Dey wouldn't hab no use for me, I'se thinkin'. I'll stay by de stuff. So she leff me. Dey didn't come for a day or two, but one mornin' I started out soon wid a basket ob eggs for to sell, when I heared sech a screechin', an' a runnin', an' a hollerin', as ef de day ob judgment had come. All de colored people war out in de streets, an' de white ladies war a frowin' down deir best chiny bowls an' pitchers, an' ebery ting dey could lay der han's on, out ob de second-story windows, at 'em, so dey had to take to de middle ob de street, an' dere dey stood all up an' down in rows, a shoutin' an' a hollerin'.

"An' den I see a great flag, all torn an' dirty, a stretched clar across de street, a hangin' way down mos' to de groun'. 'What's dat flag?' I say to a man in de crowd. 'Dat flag?' he say. 'Why, dat's a bressed flag, Aunty. Dat's de Union flag, an' de Yankees is comin'!'

"I tell you, I jes' drop my basket ob eggs like I'd been shot, and ran down de street like an ol' cow, 'thout stoppin', tell I got to dat yer flag, an' den I spreads out my two arms wide--so--an' I hugs dat ol' flag up to my bress--so--an' I kisses it, an' a kisses it, an' I says, 'Oh! bress you--bress you--bress you! Oh! *why* didn't you come sooner an' save jes' *one* ob my chillen?' An' den de Yankees come a marchin' up de street wid de ban' a playin', an' de people a shoutin', an' I war cryin' so I couldn't see nuffin, tell all to once I 'membered what my ol' missis tell me, an' I wiped my eyes, an' looked to see ef dey *did* hab horns for sartin."

"Well, did you see any horns, Aunty?"

"Go 'long; dey were, ebery one on 'em, as pretty a gen'leman as you be, sah, an' one ob de Yankee officers on a big white horse see me, an' hollered out to me, 'Dat's right, ol' woman, hug de ol' flag jes' as much as ye wan' ter,' an' de soldiers all cheered like mad.

Hampton and Its Students

"De white ladies done shut up dem windows mighty quick when dey see de troops a really comin', an' all de colored folks war out all night. A white man says to me, 'Do you know it's arter nine, ol' woman?' but a soldier steps up quick, an' says, 'Neber mind what time it is; no more pattyroles now, Aunty!' So we done stay up all night long, a shoutin' an' a glorifyin' God!"

We dried our eyes, took our roses, and went home, feeling that we had heard our Thanksgiving sermon after all.

THE WOMAN QUESTION AGAIN.

THE proportion of girls to boys in the applicants for admission to the school is about two to three. It is not unfair, I think, to estimate their relative appreciation and use of its opportunities at about the same ratio, and, as far as I have been able to inform myself, it is the ratio which exists generally among the freed people. There are brilliant exceptions, but, as a general rule, the young women are not so intensely alive as the young men are to the importance of an education. There must be a reason for this state of things, of course. I think it is that slavery has done more for the degradation of woman than of man, and freedom less, thus far, to elevate her.

Ask any young freedman what liberty means to him, and he will answer instantly, "Citizenship--suffrage--the right to be an American citizen." The acquisition of this right, with all its present privileges and dreamed-of possibilities, was a new birth to the slave--the wakening of a new soul. It is the secret, I believe, of his marvelous hunger and thirst after knowledge. Ignorance he thinks the badge of slavery. He confides in his white leaders because of their superior information.

"Look at de white folks," I heard a preacher say, in a personal application of his sermon, no doubt well understood by his flock. "D'ye eber see a *white* man want to marry a woman when he had a lawful wife a libing? Neber! I neber heard ob sech a thing in all my life. A white man is 'structed: he knows dat's agin de law and de gospil."

It is evident that this touching confidence, and his exalted estimate of his unaccustomed privileges, may easily be taken advantage of by unscrupulous leaders, to the freedman's injury, but *his* intentions are innocent. In the glow of the first rosy dreams of youth that have ever been allowed him, he honestly believes that knowledge is power. He will therefore make every sacrifice for it. A student at Hampton, asked to give his reason for wishing an education, and his purpose in life, wrote naively, "I wish to be a statesman for the good of my people."

Without this conspicuous and dazzling goal, the young freedwoman feels no corresponding immense incentive to the difficult task of self-education. A higher standpoint than slavery has left her is necessary to see that freedom's rich gift to woman is better than the ballot-box, and imposes higher responsibility--the gift of home: the right to her husband, the right to her children, the right to labor for her loved ones in a secure home, whose purity and happiness depend more than half upon herself. She does not dream that there is as much connection between arithmetic and housekeeping as there is between grammar and public speaking.

Hampton and Its Students

There is the more need therefore of patient and earnest effort by the teachers who are working for the elevation of this race to rouse the dormant energies of those upon whom its higher civilization will so largely depend, and the success which such efforts often bring proves them well worthwhile. In the list of colored teachers who have gone out from Hampton, there are none more promising and useful than some of its young women graduates.

LIZZIE GIBSON'S STORY.

"I was born a slave in the year 1852. I spent my happiest days of slavery in my childish days, and thought it was always to be just that way; but at the age of seven years that thought was changed, and a sorrowful change it was. I was then taken from my mother, as all the rest of the children was. Neither of us went to the same place, and only one staid at the old home. My master, as I called him, died, and being greatly in debt, we were first hired out to get money to pay the debts. This was not so grievous at first. We would get together and talk to each other about it, and how we were going to eat good things when we got to our new homes; but just a few days before the hiring took place, I was struck to my heart with a scene I can never forget, and it was this. There was a very public place where I then lived, and all that wanted to hire, sell, or buy, would come here, generally in court week, or the first day of the year. Then the streets would be crowded, to get them a nigger, as they generally called us, and in the crowded street, sitting on the ground, was a colored woman with her children; her husband was standing a little way off from her, crying. There walked up to him a white man, and said, 'Have, you any clothes? If you have, get them. You belong to me now. I want you to go home with me. Be quick about it, for I want to be off.' Then with a loud cry, the colored man said, 'I have nothing but my wife and children. Have you bought them too? Are they going with you?' 'No,' said the white man, 'I have bought none but you.' Then he begged to stay and see what was going to be done with his wife and children, but the man screamed out at him to get into the wagon to go, but would not tell him where he was going. Just at that time stepped up a very nice-looking man, and said, 'I have bought your wife and the baby, but the little boy I can't get. I will give her enough to eat and wear, and she shall be my cook.' Then walked up a great ugly-looking man and said, 'Tell your mammy good-by then.'

"I stood and looked some time without stirring, and when I found myself the briny tears were trickling down my cheeks. This was my first dread of slavery. Then the day came for me to stand on the block. It did not go so hard with me, but my sisters and brothers was scattered so that I never saw them again until we were called to this place again, not for the same light occasion, but it was for the fearful one of being sold. I was bought by the same one that I was hired to. I became quite a favorite with this family. They were very good to me, and taught me some of the precious truths of the Bible, which I have found of much use to me. God grant that I may continue to learn of them and become wise in Christ.

"The war came and went without my feeling it in the least. Then came the Emancipation, which was welcomed by every colored person, for it was the first time that they were able to say, 'Glory to God in the highest, peace on earth, good-will to men,' without being afraid. I could hear first one and then the other saying, 'I am free!' Then I went to live with my cousin, and had a chance to go to school. I went six months, and learned to read very well, and then went out to service again, as I thought it my duty to help my father, who was not very strong, and had six children of us. In 1870, I got a very pleasant school. This I taught one year, and then returned *home* for the first time in my life.

"In October, 1872, I came to Hampton, and will still look to God for the future."

As an illustration of what three years of earnest work can do for a young freedwoman, I add to these sketches the

ADDRESS OF WELCOME, COMPOSED AND DELIVERED AT HAMPTON SCHOOL COMMENCEMENT,

BY ALICE P. DAVIS, OF THE GRADUATING CLASS, JUNE 12, 1873.

KIND FRIENDS--LADIES AND GENTLEMEN: We welcome you here to-day, and feel ourselves highly honored to be favored with your presence. Welcome, a hearty welcome to you, kind friends, who have left your homes to be with us to-day; welcome, a happy welcome to our Board of Trustees; and again a cordial welcome to all. Looking over this assemblage, I see many persons whose hearts, I believe, glow with brotherly love and sympathy, hoping to see us prosper in our work at Hampton. Before us are some of the noble benefactors who have contributed so liberally to our school. Dear friends, you have been strong pillars of our institution, and by your ample assistance, we have been raised to this point, and we still look to you for the future. We are not yet where we want to be, nor what we want to be. We are still dependent--only making one-step toward the point we are striving to reach; and when you see us climbing higher and higher up the hill of science, you can but look back upon the past and feel that you have again received your money with usury.

"Friends of Virginia, who are present with us to-day, we hope that you will never have cause to regret that the building which to-day receives the name of Virginia Hall was founded upon your soil. Your generous gift to us of the College Land Scrip shows that you appreciate the work that has begun here, and we can only acknowledge your magnanimity by using every means given us in trying to redeem your State from poverty and ignorance. She has, to-day, many who have enjoyed the advantages of this school, working with earnestness and Christian fervor to diffuse knowledge among her illiterate citizens. Let North and South unite their efforts to rear such institutions as this, from whose walls light may beam into all our households, filling us with joy and peace. With unspeakable joy can I exclaim, with the psalmist, 'Oh! that men would praise the Lord for his goodness and for his wonderful works toward the children of men!' He has done great things for us, as a race, by bursting the galling chains of sin and ignorance and raising up for us such kind friends. Had it not been for our friends, many of us would not be here, receiving day by day an education, which brings us from the dark path of ignorance to this beautiful field of knowledge. As we go out into the world, we shall still look to this school as our kind Alma Mater--ay, a mother indeed she has been to us, for she has given us more instruction in these three years than our *dear* but illiterate mothers ever could. Girls, let us determine to work faithfully in the cause of education, that the seeds of education we receive here may spring up and bear much fruit.

"We thank all those who have shown kindness to our Singers, who are now giving concerts to raise the beautiful building of which we expect to-day to lay the corner-stone. The word corner-stone calls my mind to that beautiful verse in the Bible, 'The stone which the builders rejected, the same has become the head of the corner;' that stone upon which the whole is now resting. Let us raise our hearts and voices to the great Corner-stone to pour forth his blessings upon us, that our school may be consecrated to him, as was the beautiful temple of Solomon; that those who abide within her walls may have their hearts set upon the noble work of instructing their race; that their general deportment may be such as will give their school credit; and that after we leave here, we may get for her a name that will never be effaced.

"Dear schoolmates, the whole responsibility is resting upon us. We are to raise, as it were, her walls higher, year by year; therefore let us work with unwearied zeal, never ceasing to labor until He shall say, 'It is enough.'"

Hampton and Its Students

THE RICHNESS OF ENGLISH.

I OUGHT, perhaps, to borrow from the wit of the immortal Artemus, to head the following biography with the assurance that "this is not a goal," though it may serve as a good illustration of the first effect of disturbing the picturesque costume of the freedman's own dialect. I should not publish it certainly, if, while I know it will provoke a laugh--as it would by this time in the writer--I did not hope that it will find many readers as sympathetic as one to whom I showed it in manuscript--a lady of intellect and culture, who can judge our "peculiar institutions" the more impartially, perhaps, for not being an American, while her remarkably delicate acquaintance with English gives her as quick appreciation of the drollery of its misuse as if it were her mother tongue.

She detects within the curious tangle of words more ideas than are sometimes found in school compositions at the North, and a touching depth of heart. She sees interesting suggestions of tropical fertility and strength of imagination; she finds something very pathetic in the evident struggle for expression, and she thinks that your irresistible laugh will be followed by a deeper thought and a tenderer judgment.

I have hoped so, too.

AN EARLY EFFORT.

I was born September 1st, 1851, at Nixonton, a small collection of Pasquotank Co., N. C. When two years old, more or less, I remember loving little play-carts, and made them often, and felt that I had done as much as the man who makes the large and useful dray. Little play-vessels in like manner charmed my years as they passed. And the like fancies possessed my love. When the civil war of 1861 came on, I was near ten years of age. My father was a slave, but my mother was not, but considered free, consequently I was, as mother, what was called the freeborn in those days.

"My mother was obliged to work very hard to support her four children, father being unable to do but little. People were in confusion on the account of war, and father, accordingly, for the sake of freedom, ran away in the Union lines, about sixty miles from home, to Roanoke Island, N. C. Seven months afterwards he returned, and taking mother and the children, retraced his route to the Union lines. At first we were a little troubled, but soon father got some work to do, and began to make money and means of support. Meanwhile, government schools were erected. My brother and sister were sent to school, and I put to work to help earn means of support. After the first year, we were there, I was sent to school. I studied my books with much energy, and my teachers said I learned remarkably, thus gaining the approval of teachers and friends.

"Time rolled on, and when we had been there two years and a half, we returned home (in 1864). Now the war being closed, that terrible conflict, the people were not yet settled. Money, being scarce, father knew not what to do for the best. Government schools were set up in our city, and I went to school a few months, when father, seeking for a better situation, moved in the country a few miles where there was not any schools or churches, and his subsequent removals into similar, vicinities began an effectual change in my manner, being destitute of these necessary instructions. Tho' I never forgot to work what I could for my own elevation. Two years in this desolated land when I had passed through an ordeal of these unfriendly circumstances.

"At this point, father again removed home, and I went to school a short while in the winter, and resumed my business of farming in spring, as usual, but with brighter views, *looking on the dark, sarcastic sceneries of the past like unto a stamp by which a feature was wrought in my character, which in every way made me probably more fit and ready for incidents; which rebelled against extravagance and approved economy.* When I got these small opportunities to attend school, I valued them much. My father could not aid or send me to school much at the time, and it was my constant prayer to God for the time when I could go to school, and I looked to the time when I should be twenty-one.

"*Time rolled on*, and on Sep. 1, 1872, I was twenty-one. The time now expired that I had long looked to for more brighter prospects. But being out in the wide world without experience to seek my own welfare was seemingly keen. The first work I did to earn money for myself was teaching a small school near home. My teacher having previously given me the advice to come to Hampton N.& A. Institute, I did accordingly, entering this school October 1, inst.

"I began to see my way more clearly. God was answering prayer. Event after event with the time had been passing, leaving me apparently the more in dark dispare. Those which appeared as joy served only as the meteors which appear and then disappear, leaving you in the more obscure darkness than before. But this event was so soothing to my despairing heart, and so much more than a poor boy could expect, so lofty, *I was inspired, or seemed inspired with magnanimity*. I could love my friends, and look upon my enemies without contempt, scorn, or hatred. Here at this place I was provided with friends more and better than I felt my unworthy self-deserving. I feel with gratitude and much love toward them, and feel or rather know that 'thanks' are too small a sacrifice for their attention, kindness, and generosity to me.

Hampton and Its Students

"*Time was yet rolling* until to-day. I can only stand, compare the past with the present, meditate the striking contrast, the difference of my present feeling with that of last year this time, or year before, or if you will, the time before; I can look on my teachers and friends with uplifted, light, and fervent heart, and dilating eyes, telling the unutterable story of thanks within. My desire is to make every effort prove my faithfulness to them and my own elevation, and to show that I value it beyond my power of expression. I have every desire to be that in principle and character which men could approve and God could smile upon.

"Now at home are two sisters and four brothers, who are not enjoying the advantages of education, and command my sympathy."

THE SUNNY SIDE OF SLAVERY.

THE truthfulness of a picture depends quite as much on the light in which it is viewed as on that in which it is painted. In selecting its tone and arranging his light and shade, the artist has to consider where it will hang, and what strange rays will fall across his lines and distort his shadows. He cannot always afford to sit down in broad daylight and paint his picture just as he sees it.

I think the time has happily arrived when the pictures of slave-life may be so painted, instead of being toned down to one or another uniform tint to suit a Northern or a Southern exposure. They are not now to be viewed in the fierce glow of passion, the twilight of cold indifference, or the cross-lights of conflicting popular prejudices, but in the clearness of a day that is approaching its meridian, in whose generous and generally diffused radiance the more delicate shades of an experience that was varied, like all other phases of human life, may be discerned and appreciated.

The darkest places of slavery can indeed be illuminated only by that light from above which, soon or late, shines into all the dark places of earth, the sunshine of God's love and providence. It is time, perhaps, that those of us who have been so long accustomed to regard slavery as an unmitigated evil and darkness should look at it in this higher light. In the long perspective of the ages, we have no trouble in seeing that every nation which has been great in history has passed through its baptism of fire. We can acknowledge that the forty years' wandering in the wilderness were, to the Israelites, the necessary entrance to the Promised Land. We glory in the tribulations also of our own Puritan ancestors, and fathers of the Revolution, and are quite willing to think that the inherited benefits of their sufferings and struggles have not so far run out in a century that it is yet time to renew them. And so those who are standing as educators of this new-born nation of freedmen, viewing them from close standpoints, in all lights, and mingling not only with a picked class of students but with the outside masses, and with those whose relations to them have so suddenly changed, learn to discern the hand of God in the long wanderings and captivity of this race, whose history bears so striking an analogy to that of the Peculiar People, that they have themselves adopted that as the type of their own.

I have been most forcibly struck with this aspect of the case as exemplified in the difference I find between the freed people and their brethren in the North, among whom my estimate of the race was first formed. The marked superiority in many respects of a people just emerged from slavery to those who had not with a great price obtained their freedom--though there are of course shining and well-known exceptions to such a statement--perplexed and troubled my most cherished convictions of the value of the privileges of liberty, until I remembered it is through much tribulation that we enter into all our kingdoms, and reflected that we lovers of liberty at the North have imposed upon our colored brother all the depressing distinctions of caste that make a great part of the demoralizing influences of slavery, while he has missed the stern discipline of an experience which, terrible as it was, has developed a strength and a stamina, a religious sentiment and character in his enslaved brother which his weak-natured race could never have gained otherwise, it may be, certainly not in the tropical wilds from which it came. In this light of God upon history, slavery itself may yet praise Him.

But even from lower standpoints, we may now acknowledge occasional rays that cheer the darkness. We may gratify our faith in humanity with the acknowledgment that many large-hearted and deep-thinking slave-owners have existed, like one whose liberal views and clear foresight make him now one of the ablest advocates of the education of the freedmen, who, in the face of his influential position in the South, used to gather his numerous slaves into Sunday-schools and teach them to read and write. We shall find that there were many others who, from simple generosity and gentlemanliness, or even the mere characteristic good-nature of a Southern temperament, if you will, unconsciously made the best of the unnatural relations in which birth and education had placed them, and cast a glow of cheerfulness over the life upon "the old plantation."

There is something cheering and honorable to both sides in the fact that a friendship still exists in some cases between the freedmen and their former masters, and there are, I believe, not infrequent cases like that of Aunt Nancy, in Hampton, who, seeing her old mistress reduced to poverty by the war, insists on still doing her washing and many little heartily rendered services.

And there is, certainly, some significance in the fact that when General Armstrong, as officer of the Freedman's Bureau at Hampton, took measures to distribute the crowded population of freedmen who had flocked there as "contrabands," a very large proportion gladly accepted the free passes offered by the Bureau to return to their old homes. They knew, of course, that they were returning as freedmen and not slaves, and one motive may have been a mere physical attachment to locality, or the longing to see their own people; but it is evident, at least, that their old masters had not always inspired them with a dread of fiends who could not be endured in any relation. They found, indeed, in very many cases, that, practically, the new responsibilities of freedom involved hard work and self-sacrifice to which they had never been accustomed. And, while the darker aspects of slave life have their own terrible reality, it is no doubt true that its merely physical effects were not always felt as oppressive.

It is in the intense light of his new opportunities, and by the broad contrasts of such advantages of education and dignity as the school affords, that the freedman looks back upon the house of bondage as a dungeon of unmitigated darkness. It is pleasant to find that, even on this higher standpoint, he can sometimes preserve a sunny memory of the past, such as that below, whose single dark line, the bare fact of enslavement, is, after all, the real clue to all the worst results of an intrinsically false system.

TIMOTHY SMITH'S LIFE.

"My parents were both slaves. They belonged to different masters. We children were with our mother. Our master was an honest, religious man, and kind to his servants. He owned a medium-sized plantation. Here I was nurse for several years. I liked the line of nursing very much as it were my own brothers and sisters I had to attend to. From thence, he put me in the house as a dining-room servant. I can almost imagine now precisely how I looked then standing round the table with a large bunch of peacock feathers in my hand fanning the flies off. Just as soon as the meals would be over, I would be out playing, hunting, or fishing. I seen delightful times in those days. When I was at home, they would have me sometimes working on the farm, sometimes in the house. Either occupation were done cheerfully. Everything seemed pleasant to me, and I was almost as happy as a spring bird, except for one thing, that I was bereft of that grieved me much, and that was an education. I had almost everything I wished for in reason except an education and freedom. When I was large enough to attend to my master's affairs, he put me at the head of his farm. This I delighted in much. I felt like that he was a dear friend of mine, for he would often tell me that I would be free some of these days, for the Bible said so. This was several years before the rebellion, but I believed him, for he was a truthful man. I have followed my plow many a day, whistling of my plain tunes, and felt like that there was a better day a coming--meanwhile I enjoyed a good time.

"At the end of the war, he told me I was welcome to stay with him the balance of the year. He clothed and fed me, but gave me no wages. As my mother and father had been parted by some misfortune, I was obliged to look out for mother and seven children, so when Christmas drew nigh I told him that I must get a home where I could work for them. He told me he would give me any price in reason if I would stay with him the next year. Well, I agreed to stay, provided he would give me one fourth of everything that was made upon the plantation and feed the whole family and school us of nights. He immediately agreed to do so. I would work hard upon the farm all day and study at night. I did not know my a b c's at the beginning of 1866. I could not write my name in 1867. There were no public schools nearby. I walked a mile every night, sometimes in snow knee-deep. I seen that education was a great thing and something that I badly needed, especially in keeping my accounts. I stayed there during 1868. That fall I had a chance to go five months to a public school. I thought the time was precious and I lost just as little of it as possible. My distance then was five miles, which I walked every night and morning. Rain, hail, or snow seldom kept me back. During that time, I professed religion. Ever since that time, I have been trying to serve my Heavenly Master. I find it to be the greatest thing that I ever did in my life. In 1869, I went seven months to school again, living with my uncle three miles from the school.

"The Superintendent of the county was anxious to have me come to this Institution, so through his recommendation I am here to-day, and belong to the Junior Class. I am grateful to God for this much-esteemed opportunity.

"Dear reader, you will please remember when you read these few lines that you are reading the writing of a person that has only had about sixteen or seventeen months school altogether."

FATHER PARKER'S STORY.

FATHER PARKER would make a fine specimen of an African bishop, were he called to the sceptre of St. Augustine instead of the pastoral charge of the one colored Methodist flock in Hampton. He has ample presence and dignity for the position, and the effect of his portly six feet of stature is added to by a pair of silver-bowed spectacles, which are usually pushed far up on his high bald crown above the ring of grizzled wool around it. His superbly sonorous voice, without a suspicion of nasal tone, rings through his little Zion every Sunday, awakening sinners and comforting saints, and when he cries, "De Lord will come, my brudderin', an', as one ob de commentators tells us, 'He will burn up de chaff wid unsquinchable fire!'" wailing moans of fearful expectation rise to the rafters; and when he whispers tenderly, "Oh! *don't* you know, my little chil'en, dat my *dear* Jesus hab died for you, an' hab giben himself for you?" his words are echoed with sobs.

At a love-feast one night, in the silent pause after the wild, rude hymns poured forth that night with unusual fervor and earnestness, Father Parker talked to his flock of the wonderful peace of God that filled his heart. "Twenty-two years ago, my brudderin', de Lord spake peace to my soul. Den ebery thing said peace to me also. De birds sang 'Peace, peace,' an' de leaves up in de tree-tops said 'Peace, peace,' an' my own heart said 'Peace!' an', my brudderin', it has been saying 'peace' eber sence."

After listening to one of his Sunday morning sermons, as we occasionally liked to do, two of the teachers from the "Missionary" lingered after service to introduce ourselves to Father Parker, and ask if we might call and see him some evening, and talk over the "old times" with him a little. He welcomed us with affability that was courtly, so the next Saturday evening found us at his door.

It was, opened by a fresh-faced woman who asked us into the neat little parlor with a smile, while she went to "tell Father," who was in his study. A bright little girl, sitting in the room with her book, we naturally took for a grand-daughter, but she said she had been adopted by Father Parker, who sent her to school.

Summoned to his "study," we mounted the stairs, and found it to be a corner of his bedroom, where the old bishop was seated in a comfortable arm-chair, before a table holding two or three books besides his well-worn Bible, while a large illustration from *The Southern Workman* adorned the wall in front of him.

"I'm glad to see you, honey; glad to see you, my dear," he said, rising to meet us with a cordial smile, while the fresh-faced woman brought us chairs, and then seated herself at a table near with some sewing.

"This is your daughter, Father Parker?"

"No, my wife," he said. The woman glanced up from her needle, and they exchanged a quiet smile.

"But you have children?"

"Dey are all dead," he replied, such a quick flash of pain crossing his face that we hastened to turn from what was evidently a darker memory than death.

"You have a large church here?"

"Yes, it is de only one. All de rest are Baptisses. Dere's a great deal ob work yere for all ob us. De young people don't care so much for gwine to meetin' as de ol' folks use to when we had to meet in de woods for fear ob man."

"Have you always been a preacher, Father Parker?"

"Eber sence I experienced religion. Dat's nigh on to fifty year ago. When I got de grace ob God into my heart, I war called to speak to sinners. I began in de cabin meetin's, and when de white preacher dat had charge ob our church founded out dat I could read, he had me to 'sist in, de singin', and to lead de prayer-meetin's, an' to preach when he war away. You know de cullered people war obleege to hab white ministers in slavery times. He use' to come down onst in a while and preach up 'Sarvants, obey your marssas,' an' den I'd preach de gospil in between times, 'cep' when he was to hear me; den I'd hab to take his tex'."

"And who took the salary?"

Father Parker's resounding laugh showed that he did not think we asked for information.

"But how did you learn to read so well?"

"I learned dat 'fore I got religion, from my second marssa's little gal. I tuk care ob de stable, an' she use' to go by ebery day to school, an' I tol' her I wished I knowed my letters, an' she said she'd teach me. So she use' to come into de stable ebery evenin' on her way home, tell one day her pa heared me a-sayin' off my letters to her, an' he called her out an' slapped her face, an' guv me a whippin'. Den she war mad, an' said she'd teach me anyway, but we had to be mighty sly about it. But when de white preacher foun' I could read some, he use' to take me nights an' teach me to read de hymes an' de church 'scipline."

"But didn't he know that was against the law? Did he think the law wrong?"

"Oh! 'twarn't dat, but he wanted me to help him, an' so he teached me so I could read de 'scipline."

"You spoke of your second master. How many did you have?"

Hampton and Its Students

"I war sol' three times, but dat war when I war young. I hab libed a slave in Norfolk forty year. De las' three or four I paid my marssa twenty-five dollar a month, for my body, an' kep' myself. I war in Norfolk all fru de war. I seen de ol' Varginny when she went out to fight de Shenando', an' den de nex' day, sah, dere came a little thing down from de Norf--look jes' like a cheese-box. Dey say de debil war in her--could go un'er de water jes's well's on top. Called her de *Fermometer*, I b'lieves; an,' sir, she done whip dat Varginny all to pieces--come back wid a great hole in her. Yes, I'se seen wonderful things in my day--seen pretty hard times too--but I hab seen *His* people freed!"

"That must have been a wonderful day."

"It war a wonderful day, honey. It war like de great day ob de Lord's comin'. I neber seed anoder sech a day, unless"--and Father Parker leaned back in his chair and reverently closed his eyes with a serene smile of reminiscence--"unless it war de fus' day we celebrated Mister Linkum's 'mancipation proccolymation in Norfolk; de fus'--day--ob January--eighteen--sixty-three."

We had had to use a good deal of judicious pumping thus far, but, warming as the pleasant memory stole over him, Father Parker became fluent.

"You see, honey, dey had a percession, an' all de Union troops in Norfolk marched in it, an' a company from Fort Monroe, an' Gineral Butler rode in it himself, on a great black horse. An' all de colored people in Norfolk an' roun' walked in der percession, an' who did dey come an' ask to head 'em, a ridin' in a carridge, wid de flag a flyin' ober him, but ol' Uncle Bill Parker himself! Dat's *me*, honey! An' I went, and headed dem colored people, a ridin' in dat yer carridge, a settin' back on dem yer cushions! An' I sot back--so--an' lifded up my eyes, an' seed de Union flag a wavin' an' a wavin' ober my head--so--an' de music a playin', an' de people a shoutin', an' I said, 'O Lord! can dis be *me*--ol' Bill Parker--slave forty year--a settin' back in dis yere carridge, on dese yere cushions, wid de ol' flag a flyin' ober my head, a ridin' along at de head ob dis percession ob free men?' An' I sot back!"

Father Parker suited the action to the word, closing his eyes with an ineffable smile of satisfaction, as if he still heard the freemen's shout.

It was a climax, and we rose to go.

"And since then, you have not preached 'Servants, obey your masters,' Father Parker?"

Hampton and Its Students

"I preaches, honey, 'Stan' fas', derefore, in de liberty wherewith my Jesus Christ hab make you free!'"

"Good-night, Father Parker."

"Good-night, honey."

Hampton and Its Students

"WANT TO FEEL RIGHT ABOUT IT."

ONE of the noblest traits brought out in the negro's character by the stern discipline of slavery is a marvelous sweetness of temper toward his old masters. It was amply illustrated in the times of his bondage, and has been nobly shown since his emancipation by the forbearing use of his rights and the patient waiting for their enjoyment.

An innocent little child once complained to me, "I *can't* obey the commandment, 'Forgive your enemies,' for I haven't any enemies to forgive." The slave did not always lack that essential to obedience, and in obeying he has gained his most ennobling characteristic. His meekness has been called weakness, and so was Christ's.

There is, to me, something inexpressibly touching in the simple way in which some of our older students have said to me--young men old enough to have drunk the bitter cup to its dregs--"I don't like much to talk up these things. I feel as if folks mightn't believe me, and then, if I think too much about them myself, I can't *keep feeling right*, as I want to, toward my old masters. I'd do any thing for them I could, and I want to forget what they have done to me."

This is as good philosophy as it is good Christianity, and I have no desire to dwell more than is necessary upon harrowing experiences, the admitted possibility of which has doomed the system which allowed it to extinction and the world's curse.

The following sketch, which was drawn with some difficulty from one of these silent sufferers, is one of special interest which will call forth the sympathy of both Northern and Southern readers. It is the story of a gallant encounter with some of those cowardly, night-loving miscreants from whom Virginia has always been fortunately free--outlaws execrated by those who have a right to represent the South--the Ku Klux Klan.

Hampton and Its Students

K. K. K.

K. K. K.

(Names are suppressed or altered in this sketch by request of the author.)

"With the Ku Klux I certainly had a tolerable rough time.

"My first school-teaching was as an assistant to a Mr.____, at Company's Shops. I did not know much more than to read and write, and I went to school nights also. After the Ku Klux whipped him, he went away, and then I left, and went to Caswell County, North Carolina, after they ran me away, and commenced teaching another school.*

* The demand for teachers among the freedmen after emancipation became at once so great that as soon as one of them knew how to read and write a little, he was beset with applications to impart his knowledge to others, and "Uncle Ned's school" is no mere fancy of the sculptor.

After teaching there four or five months, they determined to break the school up, and put up a notice that I had to 'stop teaching that nigger school, and let them niggers go to work,' else they would hang me to a limb, and kill Johnson and bury him in the school-yard ground. Johnson was a colored man who had influence over the colored people, and did all he could to have their schools to continue, as I did myself. He also had an influence over the elections, and gave them advice how they should vote. They were opposed to me on the account of my being a teacher and instructing my people.

"When they sent out this notice, Johnson and myself fortified our doors. We had only two old swords in the house, but we were bent on staying in it. And I determined to carry on my school, because I knew it was a thing that should be done.

"About two or three weeks after the notice, the Ku Klux came about midnight. They awoke us up by their screams and yells, and shooting through the door, and trying to knock it down, The door was so well fortified that they could not get it down. They then ceased shooting and yelling, and commanded us to open the door, but we told them they had no business there that time of night, and that we had not done any thing--what did they want?

"They again commanded us to open the door, saying they wanted *us*, and would have us.

"When they saw we were not going to open the door, they commenced setting the house on fire. We, seeing that they determined to have us, and the house burning, we snatched up the two old swords, and opened the front door, expecting them to crowd in on us and take us by force, but we determined to stand up and fight as long as life lasted. Just as we opened the door, a very large man jumped at it. As he sprang, a sword was pierced through him, and he fell out. We shut the door again quickly. After the stabbing of this man, they became somewhat excited, and while they were taking care of the man that was stabbed, and setting the house on fire, we opened the back door and slipped out. As they saw us, they shot at us and ran us a good ways, but finally we reached the woods and escaped.

"We staid in the woods until day and went home. I commenced my school that morning just the same as nothing had not taken place, and taught all that week until out. Friday they came after us again. The way I did, I went into the woods after night to sleep, and came in of mornings, because after the first night, they determined to have us. Friday night I had some of my friends to stay in the woods with me. I was armed with a sword and the rest with guns. They came to the house about midnight; shooting and yelling, and we were down in the woods a few yards from the house. As they did not succeed in getting *us*, they tore everything up they could get hold of, and then searched the wood for me. When they got near to me, I saw there were so many that I could not resist. I spoke to the three other men that were with me, that we had better save our lives, Myself and two others escaped, but they killed the other friend. When I returned out of the wood the next morning, I saw him lying dead, very badly shot.

"On Saturday I left, and have never been back since, though I held out as long as I possibly could. Then I went down into Johnson County and taught school, and studied of nights until I went to Hampton.

"I feel as though I have had a hard time of it. It was all for the best. God only knows."

Hampton and Its Students

A CASE OF INCOMPLETE SANCTIFICATION.

A PLEASANT two miles' walk through the straggling outskirts of Hampton, among the snarling curs that go round about its uncertain ways in the evening--pleasant, notwithstanding, for the glory of a June sunset, and the soft charm of a long Southern twilight--brought the self-constituted committee of investigation to Harry Jarvis's isolated cabin. It was shut up for the night and dark at eight o'clock, but we had walked far, there was no other resting-place near, and, more than all, we had come with a purpose; so, after a brief consultation, we decided to prove at least whether we had found the right place.

Our rap at the door was followed instantly, as if by a bell-rope attachment, by a sharp *r-r-r-row-ow-ow* that seemed to come up out of the ground from some canine Atlas who had the house upon his shoulders, literally as well as figuratively.

In another moment, we heard the scratching of a match and the shuffling of a boot inside, light twinkled through the chinks of the slabs, and a deep voice called,

"Who dar?"

"Friends from the Normal School."

"All right. I knows yer voice. Luf ye in d'rec'ly. Ah! Howdy ! Howdy! Sht Gyp! She can't get ye; she'm fasded up un'er de step. Please to walk in."

"I'm afraid we're intruding, Mr. Jarvis. It is late. We wouldn't have knocked, but we wanted to make sure whether we'd found your house, so as to come again. We'll step in and rest just a minute, thank you, if you were not going to bed."

"Nuffin ob de sort, sah. Neber thought ob gwine to bed. You'll please to scuse me for der bein' no light. Loisa ben a puttin' de young uns to sleep, an' I jes' sorter stretched myself out to res' like, arter my work. Glad to see yer. Please take a seat."

Our welcomer was a man in the prime of forty years; perhaps the finest specimen of his race, physically, that I have ever seen. Over six feet in height, with close-knit, perfectly-proportioned frame, a well-set, shapely head, a Roman nose, and the eye of a hawk, he towered in his low-roofed cabin like a son of Anak. He might have been a model for a Greek chisel--the young Hercules in bronze, or a gladiator ready for the imperial review.

Hampton and Its Students

Even with the loss he had suffered of his right leg--nothing new for a Greek statue--he would have been formidable to encounter if we had not been "friends," but the "patrols" whose midnight knock used to strike terror through black breasts in the dying days of slavery; a terror some remnants of which still linger in instinctive fears, and account perhaps for the unamiable retinue of yapping curs that help the freedmen enjoy their new privileges of liberty, and their share in the maxim that every man's house is his castle.

After giving us chairs, our African prince seated himself only at our request, and, laying down his crutch, waited for us to begin the conversation, while the sounds from the next room--a dark alcove but half partitioned off from the rest of the cabin--proved that Loisa had not entirely suppressed the enterprising "young un's."

"Mr. Jarvis, I had meant to ask you to repeat to my friend here, the story you told me the other day you were working at the school; about your life on the Eastern shore, and your escape, you know."

"Yes, yes, I knows; neber'll forgit dat, nohow."

"You had rough times there."

"Well, I did so! My marssa, he war de meanest man on all de Easte'n sho', and dat's a heap to say. It's a rough place. Dat yer Easte'n sho' 'm de outbeatinest part ob all de country fur dem doin's. Dey don't think so much ob deir niggers as dey do ob deir dogs. D' rather whip one dan eat any day."

"Well, tell us how you escaped."

"Dat war de fus' yeah ob de war, madam. It war bad enough before, but arter de war come, it war wus nor eber. Fin'ly, he shot at me one day, 'n I reckoned I'd stood it 'bout's long's I could, so I tuk to der woods. I lay out dere for three weeks."

"Three weeks in the woods! How *did* you live? How did you help being taken?"

"Couldn't get out no sooner, ye see, fur he had his spies out a watchin' fur me. He hunted me wid dogs fust, but I'd crost a branch, an' dey los' de scent, and didn't fin' it, an' den he sot his slaves all up an' down de sho', waitin' fur me to come out."

"Would they have taken you?"

Hampton and Its Students

"Dey wouldn't a durs' not to, ef I had come out, but I had frien's who kep' me informed how t'ings war gwine on, an' brought me food. At las' he guv a big party for his birfday; had his house full ob gen'lemen jus' like himself. I knowed dey'd all be a drinkin' an' carousin' night an' day, an' all de sarvants be kep' home, so I tuk de opportunity to slip down to de sho' in de night, got a canoe an' a sail, 'n started for Fort Monroe."

"Where did you get the canoe?"

"Stole it from a white man."

"And the sail?"

"Stole dat from a nigger."

"Oh!--well--how far did you have to go?"

"Thirty-five miles 'cross de bay, 'n when I got out o' shelter ob de sho, I struck a norther dat like to a tuk away my sail. Didn't 'pear as ef I'd eber get to lan'."

"Were you not terribly afraid in that little boat?"

"No, madam. You see it war death behind me, an' I didn't know what war ahead, so I jes' askded de Lord to take care ob me, an' by-am-by de win' went down to a good stiddy breeze straight fur Ol' P'int, an' I jes' made fas' de sheet'n druv ahead, 'n nex' mornin' I got safe to de Fort."

"There you were all right, I suppose."

"Well, dat war 'fore Gin'ral Butler had 'lowed we war contraban'. I went to him an' asked him to let me enlist, but he said *it warn't a black man's war*. I tol' him it *would* be a black man's war 'fore dey got fru. He guv me work dough, an' I war gettin' on bery well, tell one day I seed a man giben up to his marssa dat come fur him, an' I 'cluded dat war not de place for me, so I hired on to a ship gwine to Cuba, an' den on one a-gwine to Africa, an' war gone near two year. When I landed in Boston, I foun' dat it had got to be a black man's war fo' suah. I tried to 'list in de 54th Massachusetts, Gin'ral Shaw's rigiment, but dat war jes' full. So I war one ob de fus' dat 'listed in de 55th, an' I fowt wid it till de battle ob Folly Island. Dere I war wounded free times; fust in dis arm, but I kep' on fightin' till a ball struck my leg an' I fell. I war struck once more in de same leg, an' I lay on de fiel' all night. I should have bled to death ef all our men hadn't been drilled in usin' a tourniquet, an' supplied wid bandages. I jes' had time to stick my knife in de knot an' twist it tight 'fore I fainted. When dey foun' me, dey was gwine to take my leg off, but dey said 'twarn't no use, I'd die anyway. But I didn't die, 'n war sent to a horspital. I war dar for six months, 'n my leg war bery bad, pieces ob de bone a comin' out. But I stood it all for to keep my leg, 'n at las' it got well, only a bit stiff. Den I come back to Hampton an' tuk dis little place, an' war doin' mighty well, but all ter wunst de woun' opened agin', an' I had to lose my leg arter all."

"Didn't you feel like staying in Africa when you were there?

"No, madam, I went 'shore in Liberia, an' looked about, but I 'cluded I'd rudder come home."

"You had a strong attraction here, I suppose--a wife and children."

"Well, I couldn't fotch my wife wid me from de Easte'n sho', I didn't want to risk her life wid mine; but when I got back from Africa, I sent for her, an' she sent me word she thought she'd marry anoder man. Arter de war was ober, an' I'd got my place yere, she sen's me word her husban' is dead, but I tol' her she mout a kep' me when she had me, 'n I could get one I liked better, 'n so I have."

The children having subsided, Loisa, becoming interested in the conversation, stood leaning against the lintel of the alcove, near her husband's chair, and received his compliment at her rival's expense with a conscious smile.

"Can you read, Mr. Jarvis?"

"No, I can't read much ob any. I'se worked a good deal at de Missionary, but I war too ol' to go to school. Loisa, she l'arned, an' she sot to teachin' me, but I couldn' l'arn nuffin' from *her*."

"Is that your fault, Mrs. Jarvis, or your husband's?"

"It's his, I reckon, ma'am," she answered with a giggle. "I c'd teach him ef he'd let me."

"Well, 'tain't de thing fur a woman to be a teachin' her husban'; 'tain't accordin' to scriptur', 'n I don' approve ob it no how!"

Hampton and Its Students

This great principle of orthodoxy established, we turned to the remaining object of our visit.

"Mr. Jarvis, we won't keep you up any longer now, but we are anxious to get hold of some plantation songs of a different kind from the spirituals; some of those you used to sing at your work, you know; at corn-huskings or on the water. If we come some other day, can you sing us some?"

"Not o' dem corn-shuckin' songs, madam. Neber sung none o' dem sence I 'sperienced religion. Dem's wicked songs."

"I have heard some of your people say something of that sort, but I didn't suppose they could *all* be wicked songs. Are there no good ones?"

"Nuffin's good dat ain't religious, madam. Nobody sings dem corn-shuckin' songs arter dey's done got religion."

"So you have got religion, Mr. Jarvis. Well, that is a great thing to have."

"So it am, madam. 'Twar a missionary lady a teachin' yere jes' arter de war dat led me to 'sperience it. I neber had t'ought much about my sins, no way, an' when she talk to me I tol' her I specked I warn't no more ob a sinner dan de mos' o' folks. But I meditated on it a heap, an' I see I war a mighty great sinner fo' suah, an' I felt mighty bad about' it-- couldn't eat nor nuffin'--tell one night de Lord he come an' tell me my sins war all forgiben, an' I got so powerful weak I could skursely stan'. An' den de glory come into my soul, an' I sot up a hollerin' an' a shoutin' so's I couldn't stop, an' in de mornin' I went to tell Miss Smith, 'n I couldn't help a hollerin' 'n a shoutin'. 'Why, Jarvis, you'se gone crazy,' says she. She'd tol' me to get religion, an' when I done got it, jes' as she said, she t'ought I war crazy. Dat ar' war cur'ous! But when you'se got de glory in your soul, you can't *help* a hollerin' 'n a shoutin'."

"Then, as you have experienced religion, Mr. Jarvis, I suppose you have forgiven your old master, haven't you?"

It was an unexpected blow. The glow died out of his face, and his head dropped. There was, evidently, a mental struggle. Then he straightened himself, his features set for an inevitable conclusion.

Hampton and Its Students

"Yes, sah! I'se forgub him; de Lord *knows* I'se forgub him; but"--his eye kindled again as the human nature burst forth--"but I'd gib my oder leg to meet him in battle!"

"Well, we'll talk about this another time, Mr. Jarvis. Goodnight now."

"Good-night, sah."

The subterranean terrier gave us a parting salute, and then let us go to the other dogs.

JUST WHERE TO PUT DEM.

A DIMINUTIVE Hampton student, leaning delighted over a volume of natural history with colored illustrations which his teacher was showing him, pondered thoughtfully awhile over the picture of the monkeys, and then, turning his twinkling black eyes up to her face, said inquiringly,

"Dey *do* say, Miss Deming, dat dem is *old-timefolks*."

I fancy that she did not add to his stray crumb of Darwinism a crusty hint of what further "dey *do* say"--some of dem--on the classification of folks in general, and his folks in particular. It would seem somewhat difficult indeed to set appropriate bounds to the progress of a race, one of whose genuine sons has been able to evolve as much in ten years time from adverse fate as the author of our closing sketch, and the oration which follows it.

LIFE OF GEORGE E. STEPHENS.

"I was born a slave in 1853. My mother, with the assistance of my father, hired her time by washing clothes. Her children being too young for service, were allowed to stay with her. It would be just to say that these privileges, which were rare, were obtained from a family through whose veins flowed Quaker blood--a race of people who always act with clemency.

"During my slave-life I had a desire to learn to read, but did not have any one to teach me; but, unexpectedly, and against the prevailing sentiment of the South, the youngest servants owned by my master were on Sunday evenings taken into his sitting-room, and there we would spend the afternoon learning the alphabet. I had an eager desire to learn, and bought myself a large book containing painted letters and pictures. This book I bought with a silver dime from my so-called master's store, and in it I learned over half of my letters.

"Being familiar with the fact that war was approaching, I was cheered by the hope I should be able to read at no distant day. Well do I remember when the news was echoed from one end of the town to the other, 'The Yankees are coming!' They met a warm reception from the slaves. I had the privilege of seeing the first who came to our town in uniform. I often visited the soldiers, who were very kind to me. My uncle with twelve others ran the blockade and boarded a man-of-war. This action created a great sensation, as they were the first who had left their masters. Soon after this we all left.

Hampton and Its Students

"In the early part of 1863, I went to a school taught by a colored man. The studies taught were limited to reading and spelling. It seemed to me I would never learn to put letters together, and when I was put into words of two letters, I was willing to give up studying. I studied hard, and persevered till I could spell words of two syllables, when the school was given to an old man who was a soldier, who had been a teacher in the North, and was fully qualified for the position. The days I spent under him as a scholar are among the brightest of my life. After he closed his school, the American Missionary Association sent teachers South. They all took an interest in me, especially one, who would spend whole afternoons with me on my lessons. I made greater progress under her than under all the rest of my teachers, and loved her better.

"Having been sent to school all this time by my father, and attained an age when I could be of some benefit to him, I thought it was no more than right that I should do something. I began to teach school about fifteen miles from home. Here I found difficulties that almost made me give up. I was placed among an ignorant people who I were to teach, and make some attempt, though small, to elevate; while not many miles from where I was teaching a preceptor had been hung for instructing his own race. When I went home on Saturday, I had to walk fifteen miles, and get back Monday to open school at nine o'clock. I continued my school for four months. I think I gave satisfaction, because they wanted me to teach again, but I took a school nearer home--only five miles off. To this I walked every morning--teaching six hours. I taught two sessions here, and enjoyed it very much, though it required considerable patience. In this way I helped my father to build a house, and sent my sister to the Hampton Normal School. I am now in the middle class of this school, where I trust to make myself a good and useful man, and become great in that from which true greatness only is derived."

ORATION AT THE LAYING OF THE CORNER-STONE OF VIRGINIA HALL, HAMPTON SCHOOL, JANUARY 12, 1873.

BY THE AUTHOR OF THE FOREGOING SKETCH.

"Friends, one and all, we welcome you here to-day for the purpose of enjoying with us the laying of the corner-stone of this edifice.

"This is an event that should fill our hearts with emotions of pride; for here will be erected a system of buildings that will supply ample privileges to those who wish to become workers in the great field of usefulness that lies before us; and provide those means by which thousands, directly or indirectly, are to be blessed with advantages for the procurement of knowledge.

"We see to-day among us friends, true and zealous, from the different portions of our common country, observing for themselves the work that has been done here, and that which remains to be done, ere ignorance can be eradicated, and knowledge diffused throughout this broad land. We feel an inexpressible pleasure in seeing those here who have done so much for the establishment of this institution; who began this great work under adverse circumstances in the dark days of the past, but, feeling the great need of such an undertaking, and the good that could be accomplished, went forward with unlimited fervor in their Christian mission to gladden the waste places of the South, 'and to make the desert rejoice and blossom as a rose.' We trust they can now look back with pleasure, and feel that their labors have been blessed with success, that a work has been begun whose completion will solve the great problem of our capability of becoming a useful and elevated people.

"We can only show our gratefulness to you by trying to make the best use of our time, and to prove by our actions that we know how to value the blessings imparted to us, and the avenues which are opened to us for moral, educational, and religious advancement. We ask a review of the past, willing that you should draw your own conclusions, but feeling animated with the hope that they will be gratifying to us and encouraging to you.

"We see among us to-day many natives of this sunny land, drawn by the wish to see for themselves what we can do toward the accumulation of that which is power, and which will prepare us for the duties of life in their various forms. We greet you with a hearty welcome. We ask you, under the beautiful sunlight of this glad day, to enjoy with us this glorious occasion. It should fill our hearts with a joy that words fail to express, when we consider the worth of such institutions as this, and what they are doing toward alleviating the superstition and ignorance which are so prevalent among us, and diffusing light and knowledge to all, until not a single cabin throughout this Southern land shall contain an inmate who has not the elements of a common English education. This is a result that we may all hope and pray for, and at its arrival feel thankful to God that our eyes have seen the sight.

"Our interests are so intimately connected with yours, and our general positions are in a great degree so similar, that this change must affect both races; and if this be true, why not mutually unite for the attainment of an end whose consummation will shed a lustre upon the land that no power can ever annihilate? Then will prosperity spread its welcome mantle over our land, and our minds and hearts will be irradiated by the everlasting sunbeams of religion and immortal truth.

"To my colored friends, with whom I am identified, whose interest and advancement affect mine, and whose retrograding likewise, I am at a loss to express myself on behalf of my schoolmates in words most befitting this occasion. As I look over this assembly, composed largely of those who are sons of Africa's benighted millions' and attempt to comprehend that this great undertaking is for you, that you are to have the benefit of all this, my whole heart and mind are absorbed in the magnitude of the thought, and lost to a perception of the fact; yet it is all true.

"I know you can but feel grateful to God, and spontaneous thanks proceed from your hearts to him, and to those whom he has used as instruments in this great and good work for you. You have only begun, and are scarcely yet in the pathway by which you must attain that position in life which will qualify you for the duties that devolve upon you as citizens. You have a great work before you, one whose importance you have yet to realize, and the accomplishment of which eludes your imagination.

"It is not the elevation of a few, but the raising of more than four millions of human beings, that we must work and pray for using every means in our power and improving our opportunities in their various forms, if we hope to reach our destined end. Welcome, then, thrice welcome to the portals of science, whose doors fly wide for your entrance, whose treasures are opened for your perusal, and whose riches lie at your command; enter and enjoy them without fear or molestation.

"Let us unite our efforts, for with unity of spirit, of purpose and of action alone can we make this country what it should be. Let labor be honored by all, for no nation can prosper without it. Let the elevating influences of religion, morality, temperance, and truth assume the places now occupied by vice and intemperance, and we shall yet see that a happy destiny awaits this country. Then we can look for reconciliation and welcome, peace and tranquillity.

"When we all have been educated to that standard which will fit us to comprehend the great end of life, and so to conduct ourselves that our examples shall be worthy of imitation, we may feel that we have acquired that greatness which Napoleon well might envy. Let us assume life's great duties with earnestness and zeal, and never feel that we have completed its mission until we shall be able to exclaim, like the prophet, 'Break forth into joy--sing together, ye waste places of the South; for the Lord hath comforted his people; he hath redeemed Jerusalem.'"

Hampton and Its Students

HUNGER AND THIRST AFTER KNOWLEDGE.

A BIT of reminiscence of the early history of emancipation cut from an old scrap-book, brings back to me with curious freshness the surprise with which such intelligence was at first received, even by the most enthusiastic and sanguine of the freedmen's friends.

"Passing through a sally-port at Fort Hudson, a few days since, near that rugged and broken ground made memorable by the desperate charge of the colored regiments, June 14th, 1863, I met a corporal coming in from the outworks with his gun, upon his shoulder, and hanging from the bayonet by a bit of cord a Webster's spelling-book. Already, hundreds in every regiment have learned to read and write. In almost every tent, the spelling-book and New Testament lie side by side with weapons of war. The negroes fight and the negroes read."

In the school and the cabin, I find still abundant witness to this early testimony. The impetus of the first enthusiasm for learning has not been lost, as we feared it would be. In the harder lines of self-sacrifice and manly effort, the negroes are still fighting their way out of that bondage of ignorance and degradation from which no proclamation could emancipate them. They eagerly accept what upward help they can get, and if none comes struggle on without it, as a colored preacher of Hampton, who keeps the Back River Light and walks the eight miles between his lighthouse and church every Sunday, was found by one of the normal-school teachers, struggling all by himself with the formidable outworks of an old Greek grammar, in the fond hope of being able, some day, to read his Testament in the original.

Such an itinerant teacher as a good newspaper is invaluable to those who can read. I find the *Southern Workman* in many of the cabins, and one of its subscribers gives an illustration of the general appreciation of it, with an unsophisticated eagerness that is somewhat pathetic. He writes:

"I have just bought a pece of Land and 1 Cow and one oxson, and I al so hav one Horse to make a Farm. I am now working out a Frame for my House, and to get my Head in order for bisness, it is my intrest to take your, Paper. I like it so well that I would like to hav it come every 2 weeks. If you could send it to me that way this Year I would be Glad to get at Eny Price. I have 7 names that wants to take the Paper every 2 weeks, but you must let *me* have it that way if you cant no other person, and let me know what it cost and I will send the pay!"

Hampton and Its Students

This economical suggestion of issuing a bi-weekly edition of a monthly paper just for one person, if we could not afford to for every body, has not been acted upon that I know of.

Among the applications for admission to the school are frequently touching appeals from persons evidently too old to receive practical benefit from its instructions. One such writes:

"Dear Mr. President: I am poor an nedy for the want of somebody to Teach me. I am called to preach the Gospel in the World. While I am therein the World and I want som more Instruction. If you ill take me in that Schoold, I Will find myself ef you ill find me a Bead to sleep in."

Those who feel themselves too old to begin the difficult work of learning to read will cheerfully undergo any sacrifice to send their children to school, and the young people themselves exhibit the same spirit. It is evident in the sketches our students have drawn for you of their own lives, and in many more than I have room to give in full. One of them writes:

"The chance of the slave was very limited, you know, toward obtaining an education. I recollect I used to try to count a hundred. The way I did, I took a board and a piece of fire-coal, making marks one by one. At the surrender I could count fifty; that was my improvement from the time I commenced up to the surrender. In the fall of 1866, the colored people started a little school, though they had rather a hard difficulty before they could start it. The outcry was that the negroes were rising. I went to school that fall and was very proud to go. Such a scene I had never witnessed before; therefore, I made the best use of my time. The first week I learned the alphabet and commenced spelling and reading in the National Primer. I went to school some days and nights. I had to study hard, and tried to make all the progress I possibly could. I went to school till I got so I could read and write a little, then I had to stay home and wait on my sick father, but I went to night-school. I kept up studying my books, and then began to teach school, studying also nights. So you see this is the way I obtained what education I had before I came to Hampton."

Hampton and Its Students

He has shown his appreciation and worthiness of his advantages since he came here, voluntarily rising an hour before the required time, all the cold winter mornings of last year, to gain extra opportunity for study.

Another of our boys writes:

"As soon as the schools commenced in our place, I went to school in the morning, while my brother went in the evening, until I learned to read. Then I had to stop and go to work, but I still kept trying to learn, and after a while got to go to school again by working mornings and evenings. Many nights I sat up till twelve o'clock over my lessons. In this way, I remained in school several months. Then I heard of the Hampton Normal School, and determined to try to go to it. My father said he was not able to send me, so I could not go that term, but I did not lose my determination to get an education. I saved all the money I could get, and got my friends to help me, so the next year I started for here. If I be successful in getting through here, I expect to spend the rest of my time in the elevation of my race."

All last winter, which was an unusually severe one for Virginia, one of our students, the son of the Greek student in the Back River Light-house, in spite of lameness, walked sixteen miles, every day, in all weathers, over a rough road, for his schooling, and his sister bore him company. Our little student camp is pitched for its second winter, and cheerfully filled with those who know how to endure hardness as good soldiers in the struggle for education. Our girls, too, ought not to be left out in this testimony to their people's hunger and thirst after knowledge. Till Virginia Hall is finished, they are exhibiting an equal patience and courage in their dark and crowded barracks almost as shelterless as the tents. One of them writes, in a sketch of her life:

"I feel that the Lord, who has been with me in my darkest hours of slavery, is none the less present in freedom, in trying to get an education. I work a while, and then go to school a while, and now I am able to teach, and have taught three years. I find pleasure in teaching, and think I shall choose that as my mission. I am extremely proud of the chance of coming to Hampton to fit myself for that end; and I am trusting in Him who has led me hitherto, to help me on."

And will He not, and should not we, help those who so patiently and heartily are helping themselves?

Hampton and Its Students

Sometime after the opening of school in the fall of 1871, an applicant presented himself for admission whose unpromising appearance and great difficulty in passing the entering-examination caused him to be rejected. Something unusually downcast in his disappointed face attracted the notice of the principal, and when inquiry was made as to his means for returning home, it was discovered that he had walked almost all the way from Russell County, Western Virginia, over sixty miles, and had no money to take him back, even in the same weary way. He had started with fifty-two dollars in his pocket, the results of a year's work in a blacksmith-shop, and to save this little hoard for his school bills, he shouldered his bundle of clothes, and crossed the mountains on foot into Virginia, walking forty-two miles to Marion. Here he took the train and came to Lynchburg, where he unfortunately missed a connection, and was obliged to spend the night at a hotel. While paying his bill the next morning, some pickpocket caught sight of his roll of money, and robbed him of all that he had but the fifty cents change returned him by the landlord. This crushing loss of his whole year's earnings did not turn him back. He got on the train, and went as far as his fifty cents would carry him--to Ivy Station, namely, between Petersburg and Suffolk--stopped here, and worked for eight days in a steam saw-mill, at one dollar a day, which he was able to get because he understood running the engine. Starting again with five dollars in his pocket instead of fifty, he walked the rest of the way to Norfolk, where he had to take the boat to Hampton. After hearing his story, no one had the heart to send him back, foot-sore and disheartened, to retrace his weary steps. He tells me, "When I found the General would let me stay, I determined to do the very best I could, both in working and studying." The farm-manager reports him as one of the most faithful of his hands; he is doing a great part of the iron-work on the roof of Virginia Hall, and will graduate very creditably from the senior class this year. "The negroes fight, and the negroes read."

THE HAMPTON STUDENTS IN THE NORTH.
SINGING AND BUILDING.

By H. W. L.

THE spirit of self-help in which the Hampton School was founded is carried into the plans for its future. The young men have been employed, to what extent has been found profitable, in the actual work of construction of the new building, and much of the necessary funds are won, directly or indirectly, by the personal efforts of the students.

The idea of utilizing their wonderful musical talents for the good of their people had for years been a favorite one with the Principal, but the honor of first turning to account this peculiar power is due to Professor George L. White, of Fisk University, Tennessee, under the care of the American Missionary Association.

The exigencies of that important institution had induced Professor White, Musical Director, to attempt raising, by means of negro music, a fund to save the University from impending troubles, and, if possible, to improve and enlarge it. The world-renowned "Jubilee Singers" need no introduction. Their splendid campaign, under Professor White and Rev. G. D. Pike, District Secretary American Missionary Association, in America and England, makes a remarkable and creditable chapter in the history of the negro race.

At Hampton no special effort had been made in this direction, chiefly because of the great difficulty of finding a leader in all respects fitted for the peculiar demands of the undertaking. But, as is often the case, the hour that brought the supreme necessity brought also the man and the means to meet it.

Mr. Thomas P. Fenner, of Providence, for some time professor in the Conservatory of Music there with Dr. Eben Tourjée, founder of the New-England Conservatory in Boston, was introduced to General Armstrong by Dr. Tourjée as the best man he knew for the position. Mr. Fenner came to Hampton in June, 1872, to establish a department of music in the school, and survey the field with a view to the formation of a band for Northern work. He was quickly impressed with a conviction of the wonderful capabilities of this "American music," and entered into the labor of organizing the "Hampton Students" with an enthusiasm and skill that brought them into the field ready for action within six months. While his extensive and varied experience in chorus practice and vocal training, as well as in band and orchestral music, makes him thorough in various branches of musical instruction, he is fitted for the more delicate task of developing this characteristic slave music in its own original lines, by the rarer qualifications of artistic taste, versatility, and tact, and these, in combination with his enthusiastic and Christian devotion to the cause, have in a very important sense secured the success of the enterprise. The peculiar strength of the Hampton Chorus is the faithful rendering of the original slave songs, and Mr. Fenner has been remarkably fortunate, while cultivating their voices to a degree capable of executing difficult German songs with a precision of harmony and expression that is delicious, in that he has succeeded in preserving to them in these old-time melodies that pathos and *wail* which those who have listened to the singing on the old plantations recognize as the "real thing."

Five hundred dollars were given by one who has often proved a friend in need to aid the company at the start. It was felt by the Principal that so great were the risks of the effort that without some special aid the campaign was too perilous a venture. At the right time came the donation, and the Hampton Students were launched upon their crusade for humanity.

The Hampton Student Singers at first numbered seventeen. As they were all young, and, with one exception, entirely unused to appearing before the public, it was necessary to take out a large chorus until experience should develop the most available voices. Those with whose faces you have become familiar in the concert-room, and by Mr. Rockwood's very successful photograph, and who have borne the burden of the campaign work, are, as many of you already know, the following:

Carrie Thomas, leading soprano. Miss Thomas is the only member of the company who is of Northern birth, as well as the only one who has had any previous experience of singing in public. Her home is in Philadelphia, and she was for a time under the instruction of Mrs. Greenfield, better known in the North as the "Black Swan." Miss Thomas is, like all the others, a regular member of the Hampton School, and expects to finish the course there.

With four exceptions, all the rest, of the company have lived in slavery; they are:

First and second sopranos: Alice M. Ferribee, from Portsmouth, Va.

Rachel M. Elliott, from Portsmouth, Va. Miss Elliott has just returned to the school to complete her course there.

Hampton and Its Students

Lucy Leary, from Wilmington, N. C. Miss Leary lived, before the war (which left her without nearer relatives than cousins, one of whom is also a member of the company), in Harper's Ferry, where her father fell in the John Brown raid.

Mary Norwood, from Wilmington, N. C. She is the only one of the young women besides Miss Thomas who has never been a slave. Miss Norwood has also returned to the school.

The above take the first or second soprano parts, as occasion demands.

Altos: Maria Mallette, from Wilmington, N. C.; Sallie Davis, from Norfolk, Va.

First Tenors: Joseph C. Mebane, from Mebanesville, N. C.; Hutchins Inge, from Danville, Va.

Mr. Inge is a graduate of the school, of the class of '72. He returned to pursue a post-graduate course, and was also employed as clerk in the Treasurer's office till he joined the singers.

Whit T. Williams, from Danville, Va.

James A. Dungey, from King Williams County, Va.

Mr. Dungey was free born, but has always lived in the South. He also is a graduate of the class of '72, and has recently left the singers to take charge of a school. His father has been a member of the Virginia House of Delegates.

Second Tenors: J. B. Towe, of Blackwater, Va.

William G. Catus, of Winton, N. C. Mr. Catus was prevented by illness from going to the photographer's with the rest of the class, but he has been a regular member of it until last summer, when he left to take charge of a school at Newsome's Depot, Va. He was free born, but was bound out in childhood, and, like many of the free negroes in the South, endured all the evils of slavery but its name.

First Basses: James H. Bailey, from Danville, Va.; Robert H. Hamilton, from Philadelphia, where he has lived since the war. He was held as a slave in Louisiana and Mississippi until set free by the Union army.

Hampton and Its Students

Second Basses: James M. Waddy, from Richmond, Va.; John A. Holt, from Newburn, N. C.

Most of the class have had no means of support but the labor of their hands. The young women worked in the laundry, kitchen, dining-room, and sewing-room. The men are chiefly farm-hands. Dungey supports himself by shoemaking. Towe works at the forge, and Catus at the carpenter's bench. Waddy, who is, in summer, engineer of the hydraulic works at the "Old Sweet Springs" Va., repairs machinery and does what plumbing is required.

The changes indicated in the above list have been made only by the necessity of reducing the chorus to the smallest number consistent with its effectiveness, or the desire of the students to go on with their other pursuits. The class as a whole has worked faithfully and well, and while its members prefer that no more personal account of themselves should be given to the public, they all deserve honorable mention. Their voices are their own witness. They are all fresh, and have developed and improved greatly since their first public trial.

The "Hampton Students" are all, as has been said, regular members of the school. Of the above-named, seven are Juniors, seven from the Middle Class, one from the Senior, and two are post-graduates. They take their school-books with them to improve what chances for study they can secure, and are anxious to get back to Hampton to finish the course of education that has been interrupted, willingly and conscientiously, for the good of their people.

It is often asked, "Has not a constant appearance for many months before the public injured their characters or changed their tastes?" We answer, there is, we think, in some cases, a slight injury, but, on the whole, they have, from first to last, behaved surprisingly well. School discipline has been kept up through all their wanderings; the greatest care has been taken of their manners and morals, and their health; a lady has always had charge of the girls, and the men have had Mr. Fenner's constant care. They all appear to be as loyal to right work as the students at Hampton, and most of them have turned to good account their many opportunities for observation and information.

Their severe and protracted effort, the absence of pecuniary stimulus, the genuineness and sincerity of their singing, and their high aim have reacted upon them happily.

Perhaps they have not forgotten the words of one of Hampton's and humanity's noblest friends, who said to them, "Your work is a religious one; you cannot tell how many hearts are touched or helped by your sweet music; always pray before you sing."

The story of their campaign must be very briefly told, and I have taken the outline of it from the notes regularly kept by themselves. They started upon it under the care of General Armstrong, who has gone with them over most of their routes, Mr. Fenner, their musical director, and Mrs. S. T. Hooper, of Boston, whose name is honorably known in connection with the Sanitary Commission of the late war, and in much of the benevolent work to which it has given rise, and who generously consented to lend the prestige of her position and influence to the enterprise by taking charge of the young women, as far as to New-York, after having carried through the labor of fitting them out for the expedition, at the school where she was visiting at the time. Her place with the class has since been occupied by different ladies.

FROM THE STUDENTS' JOURNAL--WITH INTERPOLATIONS.

FEBRUARY, 1873

CONCERTS AND WORK IN CHURCHES DURING THE MONTH.

- 15*th*. Washington, D. C. Lincoln Hall.
- 18*th*. Washington, D. C. Lincoln Hall.
- 19*th*. Washington, D. C. Lincoln Hall.
- 23*d* Philadelphia. Dr. Hawes's Church (Presbyterian). Collection.
- 25*th*. Philadelphia. Horticultural Hall.
- 27*th*. Philadelphia. Dr. Warren's (M. E.) Church. Collection.
- 28*th*. Philadelphia. Horticultural Hall.

"We started from Hampton, a cold and rainy evening, on the 13th of February, for Washington, D. C., where we gave our first concert, in Lincoln Hall, on the 15th. We were hospitably entertained in Washington at Howard University, by the kindness of General O. O. Howard. On the morning of the 15th, after rehearsing our programme for the evening in the Hall, we were taken to the President's mansion, by his invitation. President Grant received us in the East Parlor of the White House, where we sang for him and his family a few of our plantation melodies, with which he seemed much delighted. He made a few very encouraging remarks to us, wishing us all possible success. General Armstrong told him something about our school, and introduced us to the President, who kindly shook hands with each of us. We were then shown the State apartments in the White House, and also visited the Treasury Department. In the evening our first concert came off quite well. We had quite a full house, considering the inclemency of the weather.

"*Feb*. 17*th*. We visited the national Capitol, and saw those grand pictures and sights which I had never seen before. Up in the dome we sang 'The Church of God' and 'Wide River,' to see how it would sound. The effect was much greater than we had expected, and many people gathered below in the rotunda and applauded us.

"*Feb*. 18*th*. Our second concert came off nicely. The house was about six-eighths full, and everybody seemed pleased with the performance."

One more concert, which was still more encouraging in numbers and enthusiasm, closed the first series in Washington, and the company started hopefully upon their Northern tour.

The rest of the month was passed in Philadelphia, where the reception was fair, and the comments of the press very favorable, as indeed they have very generally been. The warm and generous friends whom the school already possessed in Philadelphia made the students' stay there pleasant. Their quarters in Market street--the old Wistar residence-- were supplied them by the kindness of Mr. A. M. Kimber, and were furnished with necessary comforts chiefly by the ladies of Germantown. Here they received many pleasant visits and favors, of some of which one of them writes:

"This has been a day to be remembered by the Hampton Students for years to come. Miss Mary Anna Longstreth, through the kindness of Providence, met the class and presented each one of us with a text-book containing a text for each day in the year, after which we all kneeled in prayer, Miss Longstreth invoking the kind protection of our Saviour over us in a truly heartfelt petition."

The class also received several kind invitations. Delightful evenings were thus spent at Rev. Dr. Furness's and Mr. Samuel Shipley's, where they were cordially received and bountifully entertained. On the 24th they were glad to have an opportunity of doing a kindness by singing for the children at the Soldiers' Orphan Asylum.

MARCH.

CONCERTS AND WORK IN CHURCHES DURING THE MONTH.

- 1*st*. Philadelphia. Horticultural Hall. Matinée.
- 3*d*. Philadelphia. Central Congregational Church. Concert.
- 4*th*. Philadelphia. Dr. Furness's Church. Concert.
- 5*th*. Philadelphia. Athletic Hall.
- 6*th*. Germantown. Association Hall.
- 7*th*. New-York. Steinway Hall.
- 9*th*. New-York. Dr. Burchard's (Presbyterian) Church. Collection taken.
- 10*th*. New-York. Fourth-ave. Presbyterian Church (Dr. Crosby's).
- 11*th*. New-York. Steinway Hall.
- 14*th*. New-York. Steinway Hall.
- 15*th*. New-York. Union League Hall. Matinée.
- 16*th*. New-York. West Twenty-third street Presbyterian Church. Collection.
- 18*th*. Bridgeport (Ct.). Opera House.
- 20*th*. New-York. Dr. Rogers's (Reformed) Church. Concert.
- 21*th*. New-York. All Souls Church (Dr. Bellows's). Concert.
- 22*d*. New York. Union League Hall. Matinée.
- 23*d*. New-York. Dr. Anderson's (Baptist) Church.
- 23*d*. New-York. Memorial Church (Dr. C. S. Robinson's). Collection.[*] *The largest church contributions made in aid of the Hampton Students' undertaking were those of the Memorial Presbyterian Church, New-York, Rev. C. S. Robinson, D.D., pastor, which was $485.00, cash; and of the Unitarian Church, Dorchester, Mass., Rev. Dr. Hall, pastor, which was $422.00 in cash, and $280.00 in pledges; in all, $702.00.
- 24*th*. New-York. Steinway Hall.
- 27*th*. New-York. Steinway Hall.
- 29*th*. New-York. Union League Hall. Matinée.
- 30*th*. New-York. Church of the Messiah (Dr. Powell's, Unitarian) Collection.
- 31*st*. Brooklyn, Lafayette Avenue Presbyterian Church (Dr. Cuyler's). Concert.

In this month, the students also sang for the children of the Industrial School, and of the Colored High School, under the superintendence of Miss Fannie Jackson. They also had a pleasant entertainment in Germantown, at the house of Mr. Kimber.

On the 7th they left Philadelphia for New-York, where they boarded--as they have always done in that city--at the comfortable and well-kept house of Mr. Peter S. Porter, at 252 West Twenty-sixth street. On the evening of their arrival, they gave their first New-York concert, in Steinway Hall, to a fair house. On Sunday, the 9th, they attended

Hampton and Its Students

Dr. William Adams's church, on Madison Square; and Dr. Adams, recognizing them, gave them a most kindly welcome, and invited, them to sing to the children of the congregation, whom he was about to address, introducing them with a few touching words which brought tears to many eyes besides his own. In the evening they sang to a crowded audience, and a collection was taken for them at the church of Dr. Samuel Burchard, who had been the first to offer them this favor, as he had to the Jubilee Singers who had preceded them.

On Monday evening, March 10th, the students gave a private concert to the clergymen of the city. The audience resolved itself, at the close, into a business meeting, and the following record of its proceedings, taken from one of the journals mentioned, will speak for itself:

RESOLUTIONS ADOPTED BY THE CLERGYMEN OF NEW-YORK, at a Private Concert given before them March 10th, 1873, by the Hampton Students, in the lecture-room of Dr. Crosby's church, on Fourth Avenue. Published in the New-York *Evangelist, Observer*, etc.:

"At the close of the concert, Rev. Dr. Crosby being called to the chair, remarks expressive of great satisfaction were made by Rev. Drs. Rogers, Ormiston, Cheever, Bellows, Robinson, and others; and a committee, consisting of Drs. Prime, Burchard, and Bellows, was named to prepare resolutions. They reported the following, which were unanimously adopted:

"*Resolved*, 1*st*. That the eminently wise and practical policy pursued by General Armstrong and his supporters in the Hampton Institute recommends that institution specially to those who see a problem of most obvious political and religious interest in the state of the Southern freedmen.

"*Resolved*, 2*d*. That we have heard with great delight the songs of these pupils, and cordially commend them and their object to the sympathy and support of the people of New-York, and especially of pastors and churches."

The effect of this cordial indorsement, which has ever since been continued by the clergymen of New-York, was apparent at once.

The remainder of the New-York concerts were successful.

To continue my extracts from the Students' journal:

Hampton and Its Students

"*March 18th.* We were invited to the house of Rev. Dr. Bellows, where we sang to his family and some invited guests, and had a very pleasant time. We went from his house to take the cars for Bridgeport, Ct., where we gave a concert in the Opera House, which was crowded, and we received hearty applause. The next day we returned to New-York, and visited the Central Park, where we saw all kinds of wild animals, from the huge elephant down to the small wren.

"*March 25th.* We were invited to sing in Brooklyn at the house of Mr. Robert C. Ogden, where a large party was given, composed of about a hundred and fifty of the first gentlemen of the city. Among the guests was General O. O. Howard, of the Freedmen's Bureau, who made an address about our school. We sang some of our plantation melodies, closing with 'John Brown's Body lies a-moldering in the Grave,' and went home much pleased with our visit.

"*March 27th.* Our concert at Steinway Hall was a very good one, and the audience seemed to enjoy it hugely. The Fisk Jubilee Singers were present, and after the concert came to the anteroom to see us."

This first meeting of the two companies was a pleasant incident of the evening. The last occurred a few evenings later, at the farewell concert of the Fisk Singers, who were on the eve of their departure for Europe; and they enjoyed a social sing together before exchanging their good-bys and good wishes, which have been so brilliantly fulfilled for the Jubilee Singers.

The notices of the city press were exceedingly favorable and kindly. Among others, the very full and discriminating articles of Rev. Dr. T. L. Cuyler in the New-York *Evangelist*, and Mr. W. F. Williams in the New-York *Weekly Review* and *Evening Post*, were of great value. The excellent notices of the *Times, World, Tribune, Herald,* and other papers, were used with good effect through the whole of the campaign following.

APRIL

CONCERTS AND WORK IN CHURCHES DURING THE MONTH.

- 2*d*. Elizabeth, N. J. Library Hall.
- 5*th*. Brooklyn. Academy of Music.
- 6*th*. New-York. Dr. Burchard's Sunday-School. Collection taken.
- 8*th*. New-York. West Twenty-third street Presbyterian Church. Concert.
- 10*th*. Jersey City. Tabernacle.
- 11*th*. Newark. Association Hall.
- 12*th*. Brooklyn. Academy of Music.
- 14*th*. Englewood, N. Y.
- 15*th*. New-York. Association Hall (benefit of Colored Orphan Asylum).
- 17*th*. New-York. Church of the Disciples (Dr. Hepworth's). Concert.
- 18*th*. Stamford, Ct. Seeley's Hall.
- 20*th*. Boston. Rev. E. E. Hale's church.
- 21*st*. Boston. Tremont Temple.
- 23*d*. Boston. Tremont Temple.
- 26*th*. Boston. Tremont Temple. Matinée.
- 27*th*. Charlestown. Winthrop Church. Collection taken.
- 28*th*. Jamaica Plain. Town Hall.
- 29*th*. Brookline. Town Hall.
- 30*th*. Chelsea. Academy of Music.

"*April* 7*th*. Part of the class visited the Rev. Dr. Garnett, and spent an hour at his house very pleasantly.

"*April* 15*th*. After our concert for the Colored Orphans' Home, which was well attended, we went by invitation to the house of Mr. W. F. Williams, musical critic on the *N. Y. Evening Post*, and leader of the boy-choir in Dr. Tyng's church. We were hospitably entertained, and had the pleasure of hearing his choir rehearse, and of singing to them. They did themselves great credit.

"*April* 16*th*. By the kindness of Miss Magie, a friend of the school, we enjoyed a ride around Central Park. It was very pleasant indeed.

"*April* 18*th*. We left New-York for Boston, stopping on the way to give a concert at Stamford. We took the night-express from Stamford, due in Boston at 6.30 next morning. About four in the morning, a cry of 'Danger! Fire!' was heard, and our train was stopped just in time to prevent the probable loss of all on board. God, in his infinite mercy, spared our lives, though the train, only ten minutes ahead of us, whose place ours would have had but for a small delay, dashed through a broken bridge, and carried many souls into eternity without a moment's warning. Our train was detained by the accident about seven hours.

"Our concerts in Boston were very successful. We also sang in Park st. Church, taking the place of the choir, for the North-End Mission School, and before the Preachers' Meeting in the Wesleyan Chapel. We sang too for the inmates of the Insane Asylum at Somerville, who gave us rounds of applause. We were kindly entertained at Mrs. Baker's, in Dorchester, and by Mr. Ropes, of Boston, and Mrs. Wendell Phillips, for whom we sang."

MAY.

CONCERTS AND WORK IN CHURCHES DURING THE MONTH.

- 2*d*. Salem. Mechanics' Hall.
- 3*d*. Boston. Music Hall. (Fair of All Nations, benefit of Y.M.C.A.)
- 4*th*. Woburn, Mass. Congregational Church. Collection taken.
- 5*th*. Haverhill, Mass. City Hall.
- 6*th*. Newburyport, Mass. Town Hall.
- 7*th*. Boston. Tremont Temple. Matinée.
- 8*th*. Portland, Me. City Hall.
- 9*th*. Portsmouth, N. H. Temple Hall.
- 11*th*. Boston. Hollis st. Church, Dr. Chaney's. Collection.
- 11*th*. Newtonville. Dr. Wellman's Church. Collection.
- 12*th*. Providence, R. I. Music Hall.
- 13*th*. Whitinsville, Mass. Congregational Church. Concert.
- 14*th*. Worcester, Mass. Mechanics' Hall.
- 15*th*. Boston Highlands. Winthrop st. M. E. Church. Concert.
- 16*th*. New-Bedford, Mass. Liberty Hall.
- 17*th*. Boston, Mass. Tremont Temple. Matinée.
- 18*th*. Charlestown, Mass. Trinity M. E. Church. Collection.
- 20*th*. East Abington, Mass. Phoenix Hall.
- 21*st*. North Bridgewater, Mass. Music Hall.
- 23*d*. Lowell, Mass. Huntington Hall.
- 25*th*. Dorchester, Mass. Congregational Church (Dr. Mean's). Collection.
- 26*th*. Chelsea, Mass. Academy of Music.
- 27*th*. Salem, Mass. Mechanics' Hall.
- 28*th*. Cambridge, Mass. Harvard Square (Unitarian) Church, Concert.
- 29*th*. Worcester, Mass. Mechanics' Hall.
- 30*th*. New-Bedford, Mass. Liberty Hall.

In this month, the students also sang in the Bromfield st. M. E. Church before the Freedmen's Aid Society, and before the annual meeting of the American Missionary Association in Tremont Temple. They kept their head-quarters in Boston, making excursions into the country from there. These tours were fairly successful. At Whitinsville, they were lodged very hospitably in private houses. The class was also pleasantly entertained at various times by Miss Abbie May, Mrs. Geo. Russell, Mrs. S. T. Hooper, and Mrs. Augustus Hemenway, of Boston.

JUNE.

CONCERTS AND WORK IN CHURCHES DURING THE MONTH.

- 1*st*. Boston. 1st Baptist Church, Dr. Neal's. Collection.
- 2*d*. Fall River, Mass. Association Hall.
- 3*d*. Taunton, Mass. Music Hall.
- 4*th*. A.M. Wire Village, Mass. Methodist Conference. Collection taken.
- 4*th*. P.M. Foxboro, Mass. Town Hall.
- 5*th*. Lexington, Mass. Town Hall.
- 6*th*. Malden, Mass. Town Hall.
- 8*th*. Boston. Tremont st. M. E. Church. Collection.
- 9*th*. Concord, N. H. Phoenix Hall.
- 10*th*. Manchester, N. H. Music Hall.
- 11*th*. Nashua, N. H. City Hall.
- 12*th*. Quincy, Mass. Town Hall.
- 13*th*. North Bridgewater, Mass.
- 15*th*. Jamaica Plain, Mass. Unitarian Church (Mr. Clark's). Collection.
- 16*th*. Franklin, Mass. Congregational Church. Concert.
- 17*th*. Fall River, Mass. First Baptist Church. Concert.
- 18*th*. Andover, Mass. Town Hall.
- 19*th*. Newton, Mass. Elliott Church. Concert.
- 20*th*. Waltham, Mass. Rumford Hall.
- 22*d*. Arlington, Mass. Congregational Church (Dr. Cady's). Collection.
- 23*d* Manchester, N. H. Music Hall.
- 24*th*. Concord, N. H. Phoenix Hall.
- 25*th*. Medway, Mass. Sanford Hall.
- 26*th*. Gloucester, Mass. Town Hall.
- 27*th*. East Attleboro, Mass. Congregational Church. Concert.
- 29*th*. Boston. Bowdoin square Baptist Church. Collection.
- 30*th*. Lawrence, Mass. Town Hall.

In June, as the above table shows, the students worked very hard, singing every night, with only three or four exceptions. This incessant labor was pleasantly relieved by social visits at the houses of Mr. B. W. Williams, at Jamaica Plain, and Governor Claflin, at Newtonville. The concerts this month were quite successful. At Franklin and Medway, the students were entertained at private houses. It is pleasant to acknowledge the generous and most complimentary notices of the Press throughout New-England,

and especially in Boston. They have often been quoted most advantageously to our cause.

SUMMER QUARTERS.

On the 1st of July, the Hampton Students left Boston for Stockbridge, Mass., and in this quiet old town, among the Berkshire hills, went into summer quarters. An old-fashioned but comfortable farm-house of Revolutionary date was rented for them, and they did their own housework. A teacher was secured, and they took up their studies again with as much regularity as was consistent with needful rest and exercise. July and August and most of September were thus spent in well-deserved relaxation from the labors of the finished campaign and in preparation for the next. During the whole time, they gave about twenty concerts in Berkshire county, by which they paid all the summer expenses, and cleared about $800 over them. They also sang for an entertainment at Mr. David Dudley Field's, in Stockbridge, and at a private concert arranged for them by a lady from Boston who was spending the summer in Lenox. Several excursions, one of them to the central shaft of the Hoosac tunnel, and several pleasant visits, were made during the summer; and at the beautiful home of Mr. Alexander Hyde, in Lee, and at Miss Williams', in Stockbridge, they were kindly entertained. A pleasant surprise party was also given them by the colored residents of the neighborhood, and they had a grand picnic at Stockbridge Lake, at which nearly thirty representatives of the Hampton School were present.

A tabular statement of the work of July, August, and September--part of the last month belonging to the fall campaign--is given below:

JULY.

- 4*th*. Kent, Ct.
- 25*th*. Lenox, Mass.
- 29*th*. Pittsfield, Mass.
- 31*st*. Stockbridge, Mass.

AUGUST.

- 1*st*. Lee, Mass.
- 6*th*. Great Barrington, Mass.
- 7*th*. Lenox, Mass.
- 15*th*. Housatonic, Mass.

Hampton and Its Students

- 21*st*. Salisbury, Ct.
- 25*th*. South-Adams, Mass.
- 26*th*. Williamstown, Mass. Matinée.
- 26*th*. P. M., North-Adams, Mass.
- 29*th*. Lee, Mass.

SEPTEMBER.

- 1st. Lenox, Mass.
- 2*d*. Great Barrington. Mass.
- 4*th*. Stockbridge, Mass.
- 8*th*. New-Marlboro, Mass.
- 10*th*. West-Stockbridge, Mass.
- 12*th*. Winsted, Ct.
- 16*th*. Canaan Valley, Ct.

FALL CAMPAIGN.

- 22*d*. Westfield, Mass.
- 23*d*. Holyoke, Mass.
- 24*th*. South-Hadley, Mass. Matinée.
- 24*th*. East-Hampton, Mass. Concert.
- 25*th*. Belchertown, Mass.
- 26*th*. Amherst, Mass.
- 27*th*. Old Hadley, Mass.
- 29*th*. Northampton, Mass.
- 30*th*. Greenfield, Mass.

THE FALL CAMPAIGN.

On the 23d of September, the Hampton Students left Stockbridge, and started upon their fall campaign, giving concerts every evening for the remainder of the month. The summer's rest and rehearsals had told upon their voices, and their marked improvement was everywhere noticed. They entered with fresh zest upon their work.

"At South Hadley," writes one of the class, "we visited and dined at the Mt. Holyoke Female Seminary. Here we were treated with all the respect and had all the attention paid to us that could be wished or desired. Indeed, one wouldn't think that he was colored unless he happened to pass before a mirror, or look at his hands. At Greenfield, we were entertained, after the concert, at the house of Rev. Mr. Moore."

OCTOBER.

CONCERTS AND WORK IN CHURCHES DURING THE MONTH.

- 1*st*. Shelburne Falls, Mass.
- 2*d*. Ludlow, Mass.
- 3*d*. Spencer, Mass.
- 6*th*. Boston, Mass. Tremont Temple.
- 7*th*. Lynn, Mass.
- 8*th*. Boston, Mass. Tremont Temple.
- 9*th*. Salem, Mass.
- 11*th*. Jamaica Plain, Mass.
- 12*th*. Dorchester, Mass. Unitarian Church (Rev. Mr. Hall's). Collection.
- 13*th*. Worcester, Mass.
- 14*th*. North-Brookfield, Mass.
- 15*th*. Hartford, Ct.
- 16*th*. Meriden, Ct.
- 17*th*. New-Haven, Ct.
- 18*th*. New-London, Ct.
- 19*th*. New-London, Ct. M. E. Church. Collection.
- 20*th*. Norwich, Ct.
- 21*st*. Providence, R. I.
- 22*d*. New-Bedford, Mass.
- 23*d*. Foxboro, Mass.
- 24*th*. Taunton, Mass.
- 25*th*. Middleboro, Mass.
- 27*th*. Pawtucket, Mass.
- 28*th*. North-Attleboro, Mass.
- 29*th*. Fall River, Mass.
- 30*th*. Newport, R. I.
- 31*st*. Providence, R. I.

The financial panic which fell like a frost upon the country in these beautiful autumn days, making them the saddest of the year to so many, affected the interests of the Hampton Students of course, and very seriously. They were, however, among friends, and at the places where they were known had sometimes good audiences still.

The weather was almost constantly propitious, and they worked hard, singing nightly, with but four exceptions in the month. They sang twice at Providence to very good houses, though the second evening was that of Black Friday of Rhode Island, signalized by the failure of the Spragues. Their concerts at New Bedford and Newport were crowded and enthusiastic. At Ludlow and North-Brookfield, they were kindly taken care of at private houses. At Newport they paid an interesting visit to Col. Higginson, the well-known author of "Oldport Days." They were also kindly entertained by several friends of the school and of the freedmen; Mrs. Wm. Johnson, in New-Haven, Mrs. Richmond, at Providence, and Mr. Jackson, of Middleboro. They sang also for the inmates of the Insane Asylum at Hartford, and for the State Reform School for boys, in Meriden, Ct., under the charge of Dr. Hatch.

NOVEMBER.

CONCERTS AND WORK IN CHURCHES DURING THE MONTH.

- 1*st*. Worcester, Mass. Matinée.
- 2*d*. Boston, Mass. Union Congregational Church (Dr. Parson's). Collection.
- 3*d*. Wellesley, Mass.
- 4*th*. Lynn, Mass.
- 5*th*. Randolph, Mass.
- 6*th*. Brookline, Mass.
- 7*th*. Newton, Mass.
- 8*th*. Boston, Mass. Music Hall.
- 10*th*. Andover, Mass.
- 11*th*. Gloucester, Mass.
- 12*th*. Marlboro, Mass.
- 13*th*. South-Manchester, Ct.
- 14*th*. Glastonbury, Ct.
- 15*th*. New-Britain, Ct.
- 17*th*. Winsted, Ct.
- 18*th*. Waterbury, Ct.
- 19*th*. New-York. Packer Institute. Concert.
- 20*th*. New-York. Steinway Hall.
- 21*st*. New-York. Steinway Hall.
- 23*d*. New-York, West Twenty-third street Presbyterian Church (Dr. Northrop's). Collection.
- 24*th*. New-York. Steinway Hall.
- 26*th*. Elizabeth, N. J.

- 27*th*. Philadelphia, Pa. Academy of Music.
- 28*th*. Harlem, N. Y. Congregational Church. Concert.
- 29*th*. New-York. Union League Hall. Matinée.
- 30*th*. Brooklyn. City Park Sunday-school.
- 30*th*. Brooklyn. Dr. Budington's Church--Congregational. Collection.
- 30*th*. Brooklyn. Rev. Henry Ward Beecher's, Plymouth Church.

The head-quarters of the company during this month were in the cities of Boston and New-York, from which were made short excursions among the neighboring towns. The concert in Music Hall, Boston, on the 8th, was given in aid of the Memphis sufferers from yellow fever. That at Gloucester was their second appearance there, and the house was crowded. At South Manchester, they had a very hospitable and generous reception by the Messrs. Cheney, whose extensive and widely-known American Silk Works make up this model manufacturing village. From here the party was taken in carriages to Glastonbury, Ct., where they were entertained at private houses, among others at that of Miss Abbie and Miss Julia Smith, warm friends of the school and the cause, who pleasantly said that the coming of the Hampton Students had brought them the day of jubilee to which they had looked forward in the stormy days of early abolitionism.

On Thanksgiving day, the students sang in Philadelphia, returning the same night to New-York. At their concert in Harlem, on the 28th, they were very warmly received in the Rev. Mr. Virgin's church, and a voluntary contribution was made them by the audience, in addition to the purchase of tickets. Sunday the 30th was spent delightfully in Brooklyn, in visiting the interesting City Park Sunday-school, of which Mr. Robert C. Ogden is superintendent, and singing there and at Dr. Budington's church, where a praise meeting had been arranged for their benefit. In the evening, they attended Plymouth Church, and sang several of their touching hymns by request of Mr. Beecher, who said that they had assisted the effect of his sermon.

They were entertained in this month at Mrs. Benedict's house, in Waterbury, Ct., and by Mr. W. F. Williams, in New-York, whose boy choir sang for them.

DECEMBER.

CONCERTS AND WORK IN CHURCHES DURING THE MONTH.

- 1*st*. Brooklyn. Academy of Music.
- 2*d*. Jersey City, N. J.

- 3*d*. Williamsburgh, L. I.
- 4*th*. Newark, N. J.
- 6*th*. Poughkeepsie. Vassar College.
- 7*th*. Poughkeepsie. Churches of Rev. James Beecher (Congregational), Rev. F. B. Wheeler (Presbyterian), Rev. Mr. Lloyd (M. E.)
- 8*th*. Rondout, N. Y.
- 9*th*. Poughkeepsie, N. Y.
- 11*th*. Westchester, Pa.
- 12*th*. Camden, N. J.
- 14*th*. Philadelphia, Pa. Central Congregational Church. Collection.
- 15*th*. Trenton, N. J.
- 16*th*. Wilmington, Del.
- 17*th*. Vineland, N. J.
- 18*th*. Bridgton, N. J.
- 19*th*. Philadelphia, Pa. Dr. Furness's church. Concert.
- 20*th*. Wilmington, Del.
- 22*d*. Germantown, Pa.
- 23*d*. Baltimore, Md.

JANUARY, 1874.

TABLE OF CONCERTS AND OTHER WORK DURING THE MONTH.

- 23*d*. Hampton, Va. Normal School Assembly Room. Musical entertainment to invited guests.
- 30*th*. Hampton, Va. Bethesda Chapel. Benefit proffered by citizens of Hampton, Old Point, and Fortress Monroe.
- 31*st*. Hampton, Va. National Asylum for Volunteers. Musical entertainment for the veterans.

FROM STUDENTS' JOURNAL.

"*December* 1*st*. Another stormy night, as usual, for our Brooklyn concert.

"On the 6th, we went to Poughkeepsie, where we were entertained at private houses for two nights. A visit having been arranged for us at Vassar College, we took dinner there, and then gave a short concert in the chapel to the four hundred young ladies, and then took tea, after being shown many things of interest. It is needless to say that it was a delightful visit. The students seemed pleased with our singing, and we were delighted with what we saw. The students gave a large contribution to our school ($150). On Sunday, we sang in three churches, Mr. James Beecher's, Mr. Wheeler's, and Mr. Lloyd's.

"On Monday, we sang in Rondout to a very good audience. The next day returned to Poughkeepsie and gave our concert. It was very well attended, and the people seemed well pleased. On Wednesday, we took leave of our friends in Poughkeepsie, feeling very grateful to them and to a kind Providence for the kindly manner in which they had received and kept us during our stay.

"On December 11th, we arrived at Philadelphia, from New-York, and the same evening sang at Westchester, Pa."

The head-quarters of the class for the next fortnight were at Philadelphia. Besides the concerts named in the list, they sang for the inmates of the Philadelphia House of Refuge. They were kindly entertained at Rev. Dr. Furness's house in Philadelphia, and Mr. Kimber's in Germantown.

On the 23d, they left Philadelphia for Hampton, giving a concert at Baltimore, on the way, to a small but very enthusiastic audience. They reached home on the morning of the 25th in time to share the Christmas festivities with their school-mates and teachers, from whom they had been separated for ten months. The day was one of rejoicing for all.

During the last six weeks, they had worked incessantly, singing every night, but much of the time not even paying expenses. The panic was not only fatal to their concerts, but threatened serious embarrassment to the school. After such an experience, the sight of "Old Point Comfort" was as welcome as to the pioneers of English civilization after a rough Atlantic voyage.

After the holidays were over, they took up study and work with their classes as far as seemed best for them, slipping into their old places with a simplicity and zest that have showed them unspoiled by their year's experience, while the marked improvement in their voices, and in many other respects, is very evident to their friends at home.

They have spent the remainder of December and the whole of January in quiet. The only concerts which have been given are a private entertainment in the School Assembly Room, to the invited citizens of Hampton, and the officers from Fortress Monroe, and a benefit concert tendered by them to the students in aid of the Building Fund, which was given at Bethesda Chapel, on January 30th, to a crowded and enthusiastic house. The letter offering this courtesy, I give below, as a pleasant and welcome example of the kindly appreciation in which the school is held by its neighbors. It was signed by nearly all of the principal citizens of Hampton, and from the Fort. I have room for only a few of the representative names:

"To GEN. J. F. B. MARSHALL:

"SIR: The citizens of Hampton, Old Point, and vicinity, desiring in some way to show their appreciation of the work now being done in the cause of education by the officers and teachers connected with the Hampton Normal and Agricultural Institute, and wishing for an opportunity to acknowledge their indebtedness to the 'Hampton Students,' for the musical entertainments given to our community, we hereby tender a benefit, the proceeds to go to the use of your Institution, and the time and place to be chosen by you.

"Jan. 24, 1874."

Signed by Jacob Heffelfinger, Esq., Col. J. C. Phillips, H. C. Whiting, Esq., Col. Thomas Tabb, Gen. William F. Barry, Gen. Joseph Roberts, Capt. P. T. Woodfin, and others.

The following reply was returned by Gen. Marshall:

"HAMPTON NORMAL AND AGRICULTURAL INSTITUTE,
HAMPTON, VA., January 26, 1874.

"GENTLEMEN: I have the honor to acknowledge receipt of your communication of 24th instant, and to assure you, in behalf of the officers and teachers of the Normal School, of our gratification at your indorsement of the educational work in which we are engaged, and your cordial expressions of good-will toward the Institution.

"I accept with pleasure your kind offer of a benefit concert, to be given by the 'Hampton Students,' in aid of our building fund, and would propose Friday evening next, at the 'Bethesda Chapel' (Rev. Mr. Tolman's), as the most convenient time and place for the proposed entertainment.

Hampton and Its Students

"I am, gentlemen, yours very truly,

"J. F. B. MARSHALL,
"*A. A. Principal.*

"To Jacob Heffelfinger, Esq., Col. J. C. Phillips, H. C. Whiting, Esq.,Col. Thomas Tabb, Gen. William F. Barry, Gen. Joseph Roberts, Capt. P. T. Woodfin, and others."

The *Norfolk Landmark* publishes the incident and General Marshall's reply, and makes the following comment, which is interesting as showing a conservative Southern journal's view of the reconstruction question:

"On looking at the names of the gentlemen to whom this note is addressed, it is gratifying to see that the two old armies are represented. The Federals and ex-Confederates who held on valiantly to the end at Appomattox or Greensboro are now united in a practical reconstruction, which conveys a good lesson to the political warriors (?) at Washington."

The Students have also sung for the veteran volunteers of the National Home, at Hampton, and were most generously entertained, by the courtesy of the commandant, Capt. P. T. Woodfin, U. S. V., to whom the school owes many acts of kindness.

On the third of February, they start northward once more. Virginia Hall, which existed for them only in hope when they first took up their mission, they now leave behind them, the growing monument of their years' work, and they go forth, trusting to return next June to witness its dedication, and insure its full completion.

When the President of the United States kindly took their hands at the White House, as they have told you, he said to them:

"It is a privilege for me to hear you sing, and I am grateful for this visit. The object you have in view is excellent--not only good for your people, but for all the people, for the nation at large. The education you aim at will fit you for the duties and responsibilities of citizens, for all the work of life. I wish you abundant success among the people wherever you go, and success to those you represent in reaching a high degree of knowledge and usefulness."

They are hoping still to find his God-speed echoed by the people to whom they appeal by the plaintive music of slave life for help to raise themselves into the higher life of freedom.

VIRGINIA HALL.

By H. W. L.

IN undertaking any great work which must depend largely for its accomplishment upon the practical sympathies of the public, it is a wise as well as a fair policy to let a brave beginning appeal to those sympathies at once, as the pledge of an honest purpose, and its honest fulfillment. It is on this principle that the building of Virginia Hall has been carried out. Its foundations were laid early in April of last year. At that time there was not a dollar in the treasury for building purposes, and $3000 were owing for bricks which had been manufactured the previous summer.

The chorus of Hampton Students had just started upon their untried campaign for the $75,000 estimated as the full cost, and the future certainly seemed difficult to read.

"Break ground" was the decision, "and let the work go on as long as the money comes in. It is a great need, and the Lord knows it. We will do all in our power, and then if He can afford to wait, we can."

The ground was broken, accordingly, as soon as the frost was sufficiently out of it, and the work pushed, until, on June 12th, 1873, the corner-stone was laid by Prof. Roswell D. Hitchcock, D.D., of New-York,* * See Appendix, Note 8.
in the presence of many distinguished visitors from the North and South, and Great Britain, who were drawn to Hampton by the interest of the occasion, and of the commencement exercises of the school, and by their desire to inspect the successful operation of the manual-labor system in Southern education.

VIRGINIA HALL.--NOW BEING ERECTED CHIEFLY THROUGH THE EFFORTS OF THE HAMPTON STUDENTS.

In announcing the design of the new hall, Gen. Armstrong said: "As security for its completion, we have our faith in our own earnest efforts, in the people of this country, and in our God." That this was good security, the finished walls of the beautiful edifice now stand to witness.

As fast as the dollars have come into the treasury, they have been turned into bricks and mortar and timber, and the work has not been suspended for want of them for even a single day. As a friend lately remarked: "There is something actually sublime in the way those walls have gone steadily up, rising day after day, day after day, right through this panic, when the largest business firms have been brought to a stand-still. It is like the movement of God's providence."

We certainly have reason to feel that it *is* the movement of God's providence, and to believe that it will not cease till His full purpose is accomplished. When the panic was at its height, and every usual means of securing funds seemed exhausted, when there appeared to be no choice left but to stop work and leave uncovered walls exposed to the damaging severities of winter, two friends from Boston came to the rescue--one with a check for $5000, the other with a guarantee equivalent, if necessary, to $5000 more, and the work went on. The cost of finishing the whole exterior is thus assured; and as I write, the hall is rapidly assuming, externally, the finished aspect, which is faithfully represented in the picture on page 152 in this sketch. It is expected that the roof will be finished by the first of March.

The material of the building is red brick, the color relieved by lines and cappings of black. It measures one hundred and ninety feet in front by forty in width, and has a wing running one hundred feet to the rear. It will contain a chapel, with seating capacity for four hundred people; an industrial-room for the manufacture of clothing, and for instruction in sewing in all its branches; a dining-room able to accommodate two hundred and seventy-five boarders; a large laundry and kitchen, besides quarters for twelve teachers, and sleeping-rooms for one hundred and twenty girls.

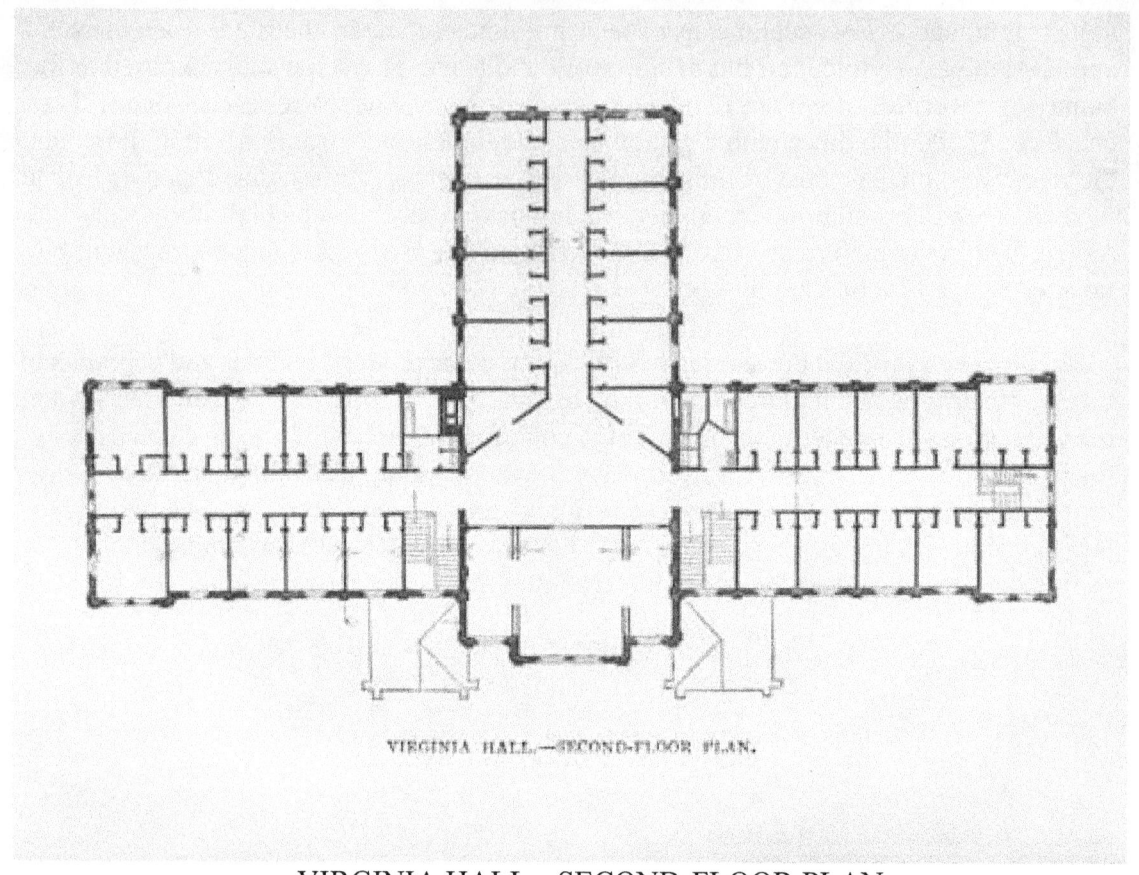

VIRGINIA HALL.--SECOND-FLOOR PLAN.

The heating apparatus is to be steam, which will be applied to cooking. The kitchen and laundry are to have the best appliances for thorough work, and are to be as attractive and comfortable as any rooms on the premises. Everything will be done to dignify labor, by making its associations respectable.

Gas will be introduced as soon as possible. The basement, eight feet in the clear in height, will be well lighted, dry, and besides containing the printing office and being the publication office of the *Southern Workman*, will be useful in many ways.

A competent engineer will care for the machinery, apply steam power to grinding meal, sawing wood, etc., and by making the many repairs incidental to an establishment like this, will, it is expected, save to the school an amount equal to his salary.

Hampton and Its Students

The friends of the school may be assured that the construction is well done. Only day labor is employed, and the work is up to the mark in every way.

Mr. Albert Howe, Farm Manager, an ex-Union soldier, is superintendent, and Mr. Charles D. Cake, a Hampton mechanic and ex-Confederate soldier, is foreman. The mechanics are about half white and half colored, are paid according to their labor, and are most harmonious, though equally divided in politics and in war record. The brains and hands employed are all local, yet Colonel Thomas Tabb, of Hampton, feels justified in saying that it will probably be the finest building in Virginia. The architect is Mr. Richard M. Hunt, of New-York City, whose reputation is national.

The institution is equally fortunate in the capacity and energy of Mr. Howe and in the mechanical skill and faithfulness of Mr. Cake, under whose care the well-laid walls have gone up like magic--obedient to the call of a people's need. The brick used is made on the Normal School premises, under the superintendence of Judge Oldfield, of Norfolk, an experienced

INTERIOR OF A GIRLS' ROOM IN VIRGINIA HALL.

brickmaker. About a million bricks and five hundred thousand feet of lumber will be used. The interior finish will largely be in native Virginia pine.

An interior view of a girls' room in Virginia Hall is herewith presented. There will be, however, but one bureau instead of two as in the picture, and a plain drop window-curtain. The cost of furnishing one of these rooms (of which there are sixty, besides eight rooms for teachers) is sixty dollars.

Will not individuals and societies undertake the cost of furnishing them? To insure uniformity and satisfaction, it is better to send the amount to the Treasurer, who will purchase at wholesale prices. The bedding may, however, be very satisfactorily made up and sent direct. A statement of precisely the articles needed, and their prices and shipping directions, will be sent to any one desiring it, who shall address S. C. Armstrong, Hampton, Va.

It is aimed to create no useless or expensive tastes. "Plain living and high thinking" is the right formula for educational work. In building, furnishing, boarding, and in all the work and living at Hampton, the idea is to surround the student with influences that shall stimulate self-respect, that shall develop the higher and better nature by a practical recognition of it.

Good buildings and furniture take care of themselves. Academic Hall, costing $48,500, has in four years of hard usage received no appreciable injury.

It is borne in mind that graduates must enter upon a lowly life in cabins, and endure the "hog and hominy" fare of their poverty-stricken people. Strong self-respect and ideas of true culture do not and will not alienate them from their race, but rather make them more appreciative of the work they have to do.

For months past, every nerve of the corps of Hampton's workers has been strained to secure funds for the completion of their beautiful building.

The first $40,000 have been given and nearly expended, ten thousand of which have been the direct net proceeds of the concerts of the "Hampton Students," and the remaining thirty thousand the indirect results of the interest they have excited, or the fruits of the collateral efforts that have been made. The workers are now upon the home-stretch. With no discouraging debt, with a consciousness that their efforts are in the line of a pressing need and of a great justice and humanity, and that the strongest signs of special providential favor have been manifested, they will press the completion of the interior so that the dedication may take place on the 11th of next June. Virginia Hall, we have faith to believe, will then be devoted to the service of the Commonwealth whose noble name it bears, and of the Divine Power that has been in all its building and is entitled to all the glory of it.

Twenty-five thousand dollars more must be secured to prepare it for use next fall, and many young women eager for education are watching with anxious eyes for its opening. It is for this that our Hampton Student Singers have once more entered the field, and that we send this little book out with them.

Have we not reason still to trust to our own earnest efforts, to the people of this country, and to our God?

APPENDIX

- Appeal
- The Southern Workman
- Speech of the Hon. William H. Ruffner
- Letters from Public School Officers and others
- Financial History of the Institute
- Extract from the Catalogue of 1873-74
- Report of Prof. R. D. Hitchcock and others

APPENDIX.

THE following statement shows the various specific objects for which funds are needed for the completion and successful working of the Hampton Normal and Agricultural Institute.

Permanent and reliable means of support are the great need; therefore, first in importance is an

ENDOWMENT FUND.

First. Foundations of from ten thousand to twenty-five thousand dollars for the support of instructors and professors. One hundred thousand dollars are needed in this way.

Second. Scholarships of one thousand dollars, the proceeds of which shall be devoted to the maintenance of the corps of teachers, enabling students to receive instruction free of charge.

Third. A general fund of one hundred thousand dollars, the proceeds of which shall be used according to the judgment of the trustees for miscellaneous objects. Such a fund is indispensable to efficiency.

Fourth. A beneficiary fund of forty thousand dollars, the interest to be applied to personal relief of needy and deserving students.

Such aid is here exceptional and made closely contingent upon merit, but of our nearly two hundred (and rapidly increasing number of) boarders, many are orphans, in utter poverty, unable, owing to youth or to a degree of delicacy or inexperience, to earn by labor in the industrial departments enough for board, books, and clothing. In some cases, those who will make the best teachers are not capable of heavy physical effort. Great care is taken to avoid pauperizing poor students, but help in certain cases is a duty.

Two hundred boarding students, in a session of eight and a half months, at an average of $13 per month for board, books, and clothes, would be charged with $22,100. Of this amount, it would be wise to cancel by charity from $3000 to $5000.

It is, in general, the plan of the school that students bear their own personal expenses, and most of them can do so by paying half in cash and half in labor, and by earnings as teachers after graduation. Much of the labor given out is, however, a direct tax upon our cash income, and this burden is to be met by the general fund of the school, which, in reality, is a charity fund applied in the wisest, most healthful, and stimulating way.

A BUILDING FUND.

of thirty-five thousand dollars is needed for the completion of Virginia Hall, a young women's dormitory.

The young men are occupying recitation-rooms, or are quartered in tents. There is no young men's dormitory whatever. Twenty-five thousand dollars are needed to provide proper shelter for one hundred and fifty male students. This need is pressing.

Our agricultural operations are on a large scale, and are highly successful, both as a means of instruction and of improvement in manly and useful qualities, and as self-supporting, but we have no suitable barn. *Five thousand dollars* are needed for the erection of a barn which shall be a model, an object-lesson, to this section of the country, and an indispensable convenience and economy to the farm.

The farm is in possession of the skill needed to manage a hot-house. Such a feature is desirable: its products could be sold to advantage, and it would be most useful as a part of our system of practical instruction. It would cost, fitted up, about $1500, but it is not urgently needed.

FUNDS FOR CURRENT EXPENSES.

Annual scholarships of $70 a year, or scholarships of $210, for the three years' course, are asked for. Many can supply these whose means do not permit them to do more. Individuals, Sunday-schools, and societies, in various parts of the country, are maintaining scholarships here, *and all who have given them are entreated to continue their annual help until the school shall be on a solid foundation of its own.*

We are putting forth the greatest energy to place this institution on a footing of permanent usefulness, to make it a pillar of civilization and Christianity. Meanwhile, we appeal to the country to aid us in paying current expenses.

Catalogues and detailed financial statements of the affairs of the school will be sent to contributors desiring such information.

Contributions and inquiries should be sent to General J. F. B. Marshall, Treasurer, Box 10, Hampton, Va., or to Rev. Thomas K. Fessenden, Financial Secretary, Farmington, Ct., or to the undersigned.

On behalf of the trustees,

HAMPTON, VA., January 1, 1874.

S. C. ARMSTRONG, Principal.

NOTE 1. (*See page* 19.)

The following is a copy of the order for discontinuing the distribution of rations to the freedmen about Fortress Monroe:

"WAR DEPARTMENT.
"BUREAU OF REFUGEES, FREEDMEN, AND ABANDONED LANDS,
"WASHINGTON, August 22, 1866
. CIRCULAR NO. 10.

"In accordance with the instructions of the Secretary of War, it is ordered that on and after the first day of October next, the issue of rations be discontinued except to the sick in regularly organized hospitals, and to the orphan asylums for refugees and freedmen already existing, and that the State officials who may be responsible for the care of the poor be carefully notified of this order, so that they may assume the charge of such indigent refugees and freedmen as are not embraced in the above exceptions.

"O. O. HOWARD,
"*Major-General Commissioner*.
"Official: "*Assistant Adjutant-General*."

NOTE 2.

The following letter from General O. O. Howard was received in reply to a request from the author of *The School and its Story* that he would add his own opinion of Hampton to her witness as a teacher. It is generous, as his responses to appeals from Hampton have ever been:

Hampton and Its Students

"WASHINGTON, D. C., Sept. 10, 1873.

"DEAR MADAM: I can not give an unbiased opinion of Hampton Institute, because from the commencement I have been its ardent and sanguine friend. I am now on its Board of Trustees, and eager to see this institution placed on solid foundations.

"Hampton presents unity in its Board of Trustees, unity in its faculty of instruction, and able administration. It combines practical teaching with its theoretical, and opens avenues to the children of the poor. Its requirements are intelligence and industry, not limited by race or caste. I invoke upon it the favor and sympathy of men and women who love to do good, and repair some of the ills of our past national and social crimes.

"God is sure to help its earnest workers. Let the catholic spirit of our divine Lord and Master never suffer it to be cramped by bigotry or narrowness, or cursed by skepticism. Then will this young and happy institute meet the warm wishes of its indefatigable superintendent, Gen. S. C. Armstrong, and not fail to fulfill the unflagging faith of its founders.

"With many thanks for the honor you extend to me,
"I remain sincerely your and General Armstrong's friend,

"O. O. HOWARD,
"President Howard University."

NOTE 3.

The *Southern Workman* is already known to many of our friends. It is edited by officers of the school, and printed chiefly by colored students who are learning the printers' trade, and paying their way through school by type-setting and presswork. The first number was issued January 1st, 1872. It began its second year with a monthly circulation of fifteen hundred, and a paid-up subscription list of over eleven hundred. This is a much nearer approach to the point of self-support than has ever been attained in the South before by any similar paper.

Over three quarters of its issue goes to the freedmen, for whom it is really intended; and for them indeed there is no similar paper. Avoiding politics, it gives them intelligence concerning their own race and the outside world, interesting correspondence from teachers, and practical and original articles upon science, agriculture, housekeeping, and education. It is handsomely printed on good paper, and supplied with first-class illustrations by Northern friends, among whom are the publishers of the *Nursery*, the *Christian Weekly, Every Saturday*, and *Harper's Magazine*.

The complete success of this paper is the attainment of an important vantage-ground in an important field. Will you not lend a hand in this effort by subscribing, as many of our friends have done, for some poor family in the South who can not spare a dollar?[*] * Terms, $1 per year. Address, *Southern Workman*, Hampton, Va.

NOTE 4.

The following address was delivered by Rev. William H. Ruffner, D.D., Superintendent of Public Instruction in Virginia, at the Hampton Institute Commencement, June 12th, 1873. The day was also chosen for the laying of the cornerstone of Virginia Hall, and the combined interests of the occasion called together a remarkable assemblage of men and women of intellect and influence, from North and South, and beyond the sea, many of whose names are honored in every part of our country and in Great Britain. This report of Dr. Ruffner's remarks was kindly furnished by himself, in response to the very unanimous request, by vote, of the assembly:

"Mr. President, I came here simply to discharge my duty as one of the curators of that part of the Land Fund which was given by the Legislature to this institution. My intention was not to take part in the public exercises of this occasion; but after arriving here yesterday evening, and finding how many influential gentlemen were gathering from distant States, I determined to bear a testimony in favor of this school, and to suggest thoughts which might bear fruit hereafter.

"The Hampton Normal and Agricultural Institute, as its name imports, addresses itself to the two great wants of Virginia at this time, the education of her unlettered masses, and the promotion of her material and especially her agricultural prosperity.

"The colored schools of the State are suffering more than I can tell you for the want of trained teachers. The lower the average intelligence of a people, the larger the work of the teacher, for he has not only *to do, but to undo*. The educational work among the colored people in the South is not only one of great magnitude, but it is *a peculiar and delicate work*. Comparatively few men understand it, and still fewer are fitted to carry it on without mixing evil with the good. The negro has many good friends who are bad advisers. It would have been easy to establish a school here that would have been hateful to the intelligent people of the State, and been mischievous just in proportion to its success. But this school is worthy of great praise. Its aim has been honest and single. Although now and then words and things out of the direct line may appear, yet I believe its purpose to be wholly educational; and the more exclusively it can preserve its character, the more useful and honorable will be its career.

"And, gentlemen, I like the cast of the school, as well as its spirit. It gives a sound, general education, together with several practical applications thereof. The royal idea in both Prussia and China is, that a youth's education is not complete until he has been taught *to make a living in two ways*, one by his head, and the other by his hands; and behold here we have the double training. Some students will succeed better in the head-work, and others in the hand-work. Some will employ the two interchangeably; and whether they do the one or the other, they will be doing valuable public service.

"Leaving out of view our new Agricultural and Mechanical College at Blacksburg, which we hope to make a model of its kind, I know of no school which so accurately represents as this does what seems to me to have been the idea floating in the mind of Congress, when it gave to the States the educational land scrip. After years of study, I feel justified in the conviction that there has been a misapplication of this land scrip in most of the States. The 'industrial classes' have not received, and are not likely to receive, any direct benefit from a vast donation intended *exclusively* for them. But this school deserved as well as received a portion of the fund. And, no act of the Virginia Legislature has met with more general approval by the people of the State than the act of endowing this institution with a third of the land fund. And the remark by the State Superintendent of Connecticut is worthy of note--namely, that of all the States, North or South, Virginia alone has given to the negroes a share in the Congressional donation for the education of the industrial classes. Elsewhere it has all gone for the higher education of the whites!

"Allow me to say, gentlemen, that although Congress has recognized handsomely the claims of education as an element in national, aggrandizement, it has left a solemn duty unperformed. It converted slaves to citizens without providing means whereby their citizenship might be a reality and a blessing. It simply cast four millions of freedmen, in their poverty and weakness, upon the ruined communities of the South. It has abundantly inculcated upon them their rights; but as an eloquent speaker has said to-day, the negroes have *duties as well as rights*, and what provision has been made by Congress for fitting these people for their duties?

"I do not desire the national government to go to school-teaching, but I do desire to see these Southern States furnished with the means of educating the children of the freedmen. Our old State has entered honestly and uncomplainingly upon the work of educating all her people impartially, and to the full extent of her means, and *she intends to keep at it* without faltering. He who says anything to the contrary speaks ignorantly or falsely. But the work is too great for her present ability. In order to do it properly, she must have large aid. And this is true of every Southern State. I have faith to believe that this aid will come sooner or later. The noble sentiments expressed, this day, in our hearing by representative men from New-Jersey, New-York, and New-England, are unmistakable harbingers of an approaching era of justice, good feeling, and mutual respect. Here we have a cause in which we have already begun to work together. And may I not bespeak the aid of the powerful talent and influence here present in securing large appropriations from Congress to the Southern States to enable them to do all that needs to be done in this great work of popular education?

"Normal, Agricultural, and Mechanical schools which, like this one, are true to their names, should be liberally provided for by public and by private means; but large provision is needed for the support of teachers in the field and for furnishing all the appliances of education. The movement in this direction, begun two winters ago, will be continued next winter, and is worthy the attention of the friends of education everywhere.

"My impression is, that this school has a great future before it. As matters now stand, it has all the elements of prosperity and growing usefulness. Let it be endowed with all the means required for its widest expansion, and, what is better, for its solid growth."

NOTE 5.

The following collection of letters received by the Principal of the Hampton Institute furnishes forcible testimony of the practical success of the school, and is offered to the public in the belief that it illuminates both sides of a difficult question:

COMMONWEALTH OF VIRGINIA, EXECUTIVE CHAMBERS,
RICHMOND, March 5, 1873
. GENERAL S. C. ARMSTRONG:

DEAR SIR: The unanimity with which the Virginia Legislature bestowed one third of the land fund upon the Hampton Institute, and the universal approval of the act by the Virginia people, afford the highest possible testimony in favor of this institution. The school is regarded as the product of an original study and true comprehension of the intellectual and moral wants of the colored race, and not as a mere fanciful, initiative scheme of education. The direct results of the institution are exceedingly valuable, and its general influence most happy in promoting a spirit of education among the colored people. Its technical cast is worthy of the attention of educators everywhere. The indications now are that the present accommodations of the school will fall very short of the demand. Such a result would be deplorable for many reasons. The Board of Education of Virginia heartily indorses your plan for increasing your educational facilities.

Respectfully yours,

GILBERT C. WALKER.

February 8, 1873.

GENERAL S. C. ARMSTRONG:

MY DEAR SIR: In response to your letter of the 5th instant, requesting an expression of my views as to the efficiency of your graduates, I am pleased to be able to state that, so far as their work has fallen under my observation, I have found them worthy representatives of a worthy institution. Those serving under

my jurisdiction as Superintendent of Schools proved themselves to be very faithful and efficient teachers, and the success attending their schools was in many cases truly surprising. The evidences furnished by their good deportment showed that, while cultivating their intellectual faculties, Hampton had not neglected their morals.

I considered Samuel Windsor one of the best teachers for primary schools I had ever seen. His teaching was after the most approved methods, and the evidences furnished during my visitations and examinations of his school proved that he himself had been the subject of very superior training. He is now the principal of a flourishing graded school of about two hundred pupils.

If such is a fair specimen of the teachers you turn out at Hampton, the country has much to hope for in the continued prosperity of your institution. The great want of our colored schools is properly-trained colored teachers.

Wishing you abundant success in your important work, I am,
Very truly yours,

L. R. HOLLAND,
Superintendent Schools.

FRANKLIN DEPOT,
SUSQUEHANNA CO., VA., Jan. 22, 1873.

GENERAL S. C. ARMSTRONG:

DEAR SIR: Yours of the 2d instant was received some time ago, and in reply I must say that it will give me much pleasure to give you what information I possess regarding my experience with the teachers sent from your institution.

I have been fortunate enough to receive four of five of them--namely, William H. Lee, George W. Lattimore, William Barrett, and John K. Britt. The course of study, as pursued at the Hampton Normal and Agricultural Institute, is admirably adapted for the preparation of teachers for our colored schools, and in my opinion is fulfilling its mission to the satisfaction of all concerned. So far as the qualifications of the teachers named are concerned, there is no question, for a visit to their schools only convinces me of their proficiency for their duties; and I have come to regard it as useless to examine any candidate for a teacher's certificate who can produce the diploma from your Institute.

Very respectfully,

JAMES F. BRYANT,
Superintendent Schools, etc.

SEVEN-MILE FORD, VA., Jan. 13, 1873.

GENERAL S. C. ARMSTRONG:

Hampton and Its Students

DEAR SIR: I have been superintending schools here for more than two years, and I have been able to get no teachers that have been serviceable to the colored race, save those who have been educated at Hampton. I will except one who was educated at New-York. The colored teachers from your school have been well instructed in all the rudimentary branches taught in our public schools; in fact, better than many white teachers who are employed in our schools. Your graduates and undergraduates have been properly trained in morals, etc., and their influence is perceptible in the schools where they teach. Joseph D. Giles, James Ricks, and Stephen A. Ricks did me good service last year. S. A. Ricks is still teaching. I wish I had more of your pupils for my colored schools. The negro race must be educated in the common English branches if they are to make citizens in the government. Our free institutions demand it. We must have an intelligent citizenship if we are to have a happy, strong, and prosperous government.

Very respectfully,

D. C. MILLER,
Superintendent Schools, Smith Co.

The following letter from Prof. Joynes, of Washington and Lee University, Virginia, is, although personal and not intended for publication, inserted here as a valuable part of the cumulative evidence offered in this book of the sincere and kind welcome extended by representative Southern men to honest and earnest efforts for the freedmen. Prof. Joynes will, we hope, excuse the liberty taken with his generous and friendly letter:

WASHINGTON AND LEE UNIVERSITY,
LEXINGTON, VA., Jan. 19, 1874

GENERAL S. C. ARMSTRONG:

DEAR SIR: I have received, through my friend, Rev. George F. Adams, your kind invitation that I should visit the Hampton Normal School, and especially at its next commencement. I regret that it is not in my power to make any positive appointment to this effect, but I assure you I shall lose no opportunity of visiting your school, and expressing thereby, personally, my deep interest in its work.

Permit me to assure you that I have, from the beginning, looked with deepest interest upon your school and its work. I think you are engaged in an experiment which has the closest and profoundest relation to the great question of *the races* in our country; and I regard the work which your school is doing as more important for the colored race than any political legislation whatsoever. Increased knowledge and intelligence--the knowledge and intelligence that add *value* as well as *dignity* to labor, and increase as well as justify the sentiment of personal self-respect; the experience that these gifts are to be acquired (for colored as well as for white) only by effort, self-sacrifice, and personal worth; and the great lesson which you are teaching, that the *moral* enfranchisement and progress of the colored race can be won only through the colored race itself--these are truths that are worth more than any mere political doctrines. And your school is teaching them by example and by precept, in a manner that must make it a centre of the deepest interest, alike for all educators and for all patriots.

Permit me to add that it is, I believe, a sentiment of general and just congratulation among Virginians, that a work so important and critical should be in the hands of a man as judicious, as liberal, and as conservative as yourself; and that our people regard you with the utmost confidence and respect.

I regret once more that I cannot now promise to accept your invitation, but I trust I shall at least have the pleasure of meeting you at Norfolk.

Very respectfully,

EDWARD S. JOYNES.

NOTE 6.

FINANCIAL HISTORY OF THE INSTITUTE.

The financial affairs of the Institute are in charge of Gen. J. F. B. Marshall, who has had thirty years of active business experience, and was, during the late war, Paymaster-General of the State of Massachusetts. He has given heavy bonds for the faithful performance of his duty, and has organized a thorough system of accounts showing the precise financial condition of every department of the school, and the debits and credits of each student, which, though involving great labor, has been most satisfactory to those who have examined his books, and justifies the school's claim to a faithful stewardship of funds intrusted to it.

His daily practical and theoretical instruction of students in book-keeping gives them many of the advantages of a Business College. The following is an extract from his report as Treasurer:

The property comprising the Normal School premises was purchased by the American Missionary Association in June, 1867. It originally contained one hundred and sixty-five acres of land, of which forty acres were in outlying lots, and afterward sold to freedmen. The cost of the land was nineteen thousand dollars, ten thousand of which were appropriated for the purpose by the trustees of the Avery Fund, a large bequest left by Mr. Avery, of Pittsburg, Pa., for the education of freedmen in the United States and Canada.

The Property is now, owned and controlled by the Board of Trustees.

The outlays from the beginning, for buildings, furniture, stock, implements, books, apparatus, and current expenses, with the exception of the amount paid by the students, have been met from appropriations by the American Missionary Association, the Freedmen's Bureau, the Peabody Fund, the State Agricultural College Land Fund, and private donations of friends of the enterprise, as shown by the following statement of

RECEIPTS AND EXPENDITURES OF THE HAMPTON NORMAL AND AGRICULTURAL INSTITUTE FROM ITS ORGANIZATION TO JUNE 30, 1873.

Receipts.

- 1. From American Missionary Association, ... $34,600 00
- 2. From Societies and individuals through A. M. A., ... 21,378 16
- 3. From Bureau of Refugees, Freedmen and Abandoned Lands, ... 58,327 89
- 4. From Interest of Endowment Fund, ... 2,244 34
- 5. From Interest of State Agricultural College Land Fund, ... 7,480 50
- 6. From Trustees of Peabody Fund, ... 3,400 00
- 7. From "Hampton Students" (vocalists), ... 10,971 30
- 8. From Other sources, ... 89,623 86
- 9. From Donations for Endowment Fund, ... 43,941 12
- $271,967 27

Expenditures.

- 1. *For Farm*--namely:
  For land, buildings, and expenses, ... $27,648 79
- For implements, wagons, carts, etc., ... 1,533 09
- For stock: horses, mules, cows, etc., ... 3,465 90
- 2. For subsistence of students and teachers, ... 38,394 89
- 3. For school-buildings, ... 83,721 59
- 4. For salaries, apparatus, and current expenses, ... 61,522 00
- 5. For furniture, ... 7,726 39
- 6. For investment of Endowment Fund, ... 42,922 20
- $266,934 85
- Balance in hands of Treasurer, ... 5,032 42
- $271,967 27

STATEMENT OF THE REAL AND PERSONAL PROPERTY BELONGING TO THE HAMPTON NORMAL AND AGRICULTURAL INSTITUTE.

Real Estate.

- Farm 110 acres, with barns, etc., inclosed, worth say,[*] . . . . . $25,000 00 *Not including 72 acres purchased with the Land Scrip Fund.
- School premises, say 10 acres, valued at 5,000 00
- Academic Hall--class-rooms, offices, etc., cost 48,552 97
- Teachers' Home--residence of teachers and principal, valued at 5,000 00
- Griggs Hall--residence of matron, and girls' dormitory, valued at 6,000 00
- Barracks--industrial-room, dining-hall, dormitories, etc., valued at 2,500 00
- Butler School, occupied as county school (preparatory), ... 3,000 00
- Farm-house--residence of farm manager and treasurer, cost 3,975 50
- New wharf, cost 916 82
- Virginia Hall (unfinished, to cost $75,000) to date 14,008 12
- $113,953 41

Personal Property.

- Farm stock, comprising one Canadian stallion, one pure Ayrshire bull, fifteen cows, four farm-horses, five mules, two yoke of oxen, swine, and poultry, ... $3,465 90
- Farm implements--wagons, plows, etc., ... 1,533 09
- Furniture of school-rooms, dormitories, etc., at appraisal of cash value, ... 7,726 39
- Books and apparatus, ... 1,040 33
- Printing-office--presses, type, etc., ... 4,899 58
- $18,665 29

Endowment Fund.

- The Endowment Fund, invested in First Mortgage Bonds, United States Currency Bonds, stocks and shares, amounts to $38,829.75

NOTE.--Rev. T. K. Fessenden, Financial Secretary of the Board of Trustees, had paid in, up to November 15th, 1873, the date of his last quarterly report, in cash and material, inclusive of collections for Building Fund and current expense accounts, $73,503.83.

He has secured, in addition, a large amount in pledges and legacies, not less than $40,000, which will, in time, be paid in.

NOTE 7. (*See page 57.*)

The following extracts from the Catalogue of 1873-4 are published for the information of those interested:

INSTRUCTORS AND THEIR SPECIAL OR PRINCIPAL BRANCHES OF INSTRUCTION.

S. C. ARMSTRONG, Principal, Moral Science and Civil Government.

J. F. B. MARSHALL, Treasurer and Acting Assistant Principal, Book-keeping.

Academic Department.--JOHN H. LARRY, in charge, Natural Science and Elocution and Drill; MARY F. MACKIE, Mathematics; AMELIA TYLER, Grammar and Composition; ELIZABETH H. BREWER, Ancient History and Physical Geography; MARY HUNGERFORD, Reading and United States History; HELEN W. LUDLOW, English Literature; JULIA E. REMINGTON, Geography and Map Drawing; NATHALIE LORD, Reading; M. C. KIMBER, Writing and Physiology.

Musical Department.--THOMAS P. FENNER, in charge; ETHIE K. FENNER, Assistant.

Girls' Industrial Department.--S. H. FENNER, in charge.

Housework and Boarding Department.--SUSAN P. HARROLD, Matron; C. L. MACKIE, Steward and Hospital Department.

Agricultural Department.--ALBERT HOWE, in charge.

GEORGE DIXON, Lecturer on Agriculture.

Mechanical Department.--JOHN H. LARRY, in charge.

Printing-Office.--W. J. BUTTERFIELD, in charge.

STUDENTS.

Whole number, 226. Young men, 149; young women, 77. Seniors, 27; Middlers, 76 (3 sections); Juniors, 98 (3 sections); Preparatory, 23; Post-Graduates, 2. Average age, 18.

COURSES OF STUDY.

The courses of study embrace three years, and include--

NORMAL COURSE.

- *Language.*--Spelling, Reading, Sentence-Making, English Grammar, Analysis, Rhetoric, Composition, Elocution.
- *Mathematics.*--Mental Arithmetic, Written Arithmetic, Algebra, Geometry, Mathematical Drawing.
- *History.*--History of United States, History of England--Readings from English writers. Universal History.

- *Natural Science.*--Geography--Map-drawing, Physical Geography, Natural History, Natural Philosophy, Physiology, Botany.
- *Miscellaneous.*--Science of Civil Government, Moral Science, Bible Lessons, Drill in Teaching, Principles of Business, Vocal Training, Instrumental Music.

AGRICULTURAL COURSE.

Studies of the Normal Course at discretion. Lectures on the following courses: Formation of Soils, Rotation of Crops, Management of Stock, Fruit Culture, Cultivation of Crops, Drainage, Market Gardening, Meteorology, Practical Instruction in the routine of Farming and Market Gardening.

COMMERCIAL COURSE.

Studies of the Normal Course at discretion. Instruction in Book-keeping, Single and Double Entry, in Business Letters, Contracts, Account of Sales, and other Business and Legal Papers, and in Commercial Law. Each student is required to keep his account current with the Institute in proper form.

MECHANICAL COURSE.

Studies of the Normal Course at discretion. Practical Instruction in the different varieties of Sewing-Machines in use, in household industries, and in the following: Penmanship, Free Hand Drawing, Mechanical Drawing, Printing.

Lectures are given through the year on Agricultural topics. Arrangements are being made to secure every year the services of leading literary and scientific men in a Lecture Course that shall afford the highest order of entertainment and instruction.

EXPENSES AND LABOR.

- Board, per month, ... $8 00
- Washing and lights, per month, ... 1 00
- Fuel, per month, ... 75
- Use of furniture, per month, ... 25
- $10 00

Clothing and books extra, to be paid for in cash.

Hampton and Its Students

Able-bodied young men and women over eighteen years of age are expected to pay half in cash and half in work; that is, $5 per month in cash, and to work out the balance. Boys and girls of eighteen years and less are required to pay $6 per month. *Students are held responsible for all balances against them that they may not have worked out.*

The amount of profitable labor being limited, it is desired to extend its advantages as far as possible; hence only those who are absolutely unable to pay any thing in cash are allowed to work out their whole expenses. Young men and women, whose parents desire that they shall not be taken out of school to work, may, upon the payment of $10 per month, attend school without interruption, but will nevertheless be required to work on Saturdays, at such hours as may be assigned them. LABOR IS REQUIRED OF ALL, for purposes of discipline and instruction. To this end, day scholars are expected to labor at the rate of an hour per day, at such industries as may be assigned them.

Bills are made out and are payable at the end of the month. The regular cash payment is to be *monthly, in advance.*

The regular annual tuition fee of the institution is seventy dollars. Students are not required to pay this. As the amount has to be secured by the Trustees, by solicitation among the friends of education, students are called upon annually to write letters to their benefactors.

DISCIPLINE.

Courtesy and mutual forbearance are expected of both pupils and teachers, as indispensable to good discipline.

Every student is by enrollment committed to the discipline and regulations of the school.

Students are subject to suspension or discharge for an unsatisfactory course in respect to study, conduct, or labor.

The use of ardent spirits and tobacco is prohibited. Letter-writing is subject to regulation.

The wardrobes of all students are subject to inspection and regulation by the proper officers.

Students are subject to drill and guard duty. Obedience to the Commandant must be implicit. The rights of students are properly guarded.

DAILY ORDER OF EXERCISES AT THE H. N. AND A. INSTITUTE.

- A. M.--5.00 Rising Bell.
- A. M.--5.45 Inspection of Men.
- A. M.--6.00 Breakfast.
- A. M.--6.30 Family Prayers.
- A. M.--8.00 Inspection of quarters.
- A. M.--8.30 Opening of school. Roll Call and Exercises.
- A. M.--8.55 to 10.20 Classes in Reading, Natural Philosophy, Arithmetic, Grammar, Geography, and Bookkeeping.
- A. M.--10.20 to 10.40 Recess.
- A. M.--10.40 to 12.15 Classes in Writing, Arithmetic, Grammar, History, Algebra, and Elocution.
- P. M.--12.15 to 1.30 Dinner and intermission.
- P. M.--1:30 Roll Call.
- P. M.--1.40 to 2.50 Classes in Spelling, Arithmetic, Grammar, Geography, Natural Philosophy, History, Civil Government, and Moral Science.
- P. M.--4.00 Cadet Drill.
- P. M.--6.00 Supper.
- P. M.--6.45 Evening Prayers.
- P. M.--7.15 to 9 Evening Study Hours.
- P. M.--9.30 Retiring Bell.

On Sunday there are morning religious services in the Chapel, conducted by the Rev. Richard Tolman, formerly of Tewksbury, Mass., who has pastoral charge of the school. The Church is organized as the "Bethesda Church," and has no denominational name or connection. Sunday afternoon there are Bible-Classes in the Assembly Hall, and in the evening a lecture or prayer meeting.

NOTE 8.

Report of the Committee of Visitors to the School at its Commencement, June 12th, 1873:

By invitation of the Trustees of the Hampton Normal School, the undersigned attended the Commencement exercises of that institution on Thursday, June 12th, 1873.

Hampton and Its Students

A detailed report might easily have been provided for, but the end contemplated may perhaps be better served by a general statement of the impressions made upon us.

The location of the institution seemed to us every way most felicitous. The scenery is of a subdued and quiet type, but very charming. The historic associations, both remote and recent, are suggestive and stimulating.

The whole spirit of the institution is at the widest possible remove from everything extravagant and fanatical. The colored race are not overrated, either morally or intellectually. On the contrary, their characteristic infirmities are distinctly recognized, and diligently combated. Consequently the immediate neighbors of the institution, and the white people of Virginia generally, as they come to understand the matter, are more and more friendly from year to year. Self-interest of course dictates the education of a race which has been so suddenly enfranchised; but along with this there is likewise a great deal of the old Anglo-Saxon love of fair play, and the negroes admit they will have themselves only to blame, if they go to the wall.

The institution is singularly happy in its corps of instructors. General Armstrong has a combination of qualities which fit him admirably for his position. He has great enthusiasm and great diligence in his work. The teachers under him are much above the average. The recitations we heard gave proof of very thorough and very skillful drilling. Such eagerness for knowledge, on the part of pupils, we never saw before. It seemed to us like a long thirst just beginning to be satisfied. The five canvas tents upon the lawn looked as gallant as any tents ever did on a battle-field.

But the institution has not yet reached half its proper stature. The new building, whose corner-stone we assisted in laying, is most urgently needed. Men of property can make no better use of it than at Hampton, in strengthening an institution which, though it may have rivals, as we hope it may, is not likely to be surpassed by any similar institution anywhere in the South.

ROSWELL D. HITCHCOCK,
HENRY W. BELLOWS,
WILLIAM I. BUDINGTON,
WILLIAM M. TAYLOR.

NEW YORK, January, 1874.

CABIN AND PLANTATION SONGS, AS SUNG BY THE HAMPTON STUDENTS.

CABIN AND PLANTATION SONGS, AS SUNG BY THE HAMPTON STUDENTS.

ARRANGED BY

THOMAS P. FENNER,

IN CHARGE OF MUSICAL DEPARTMENT AT HAMPTON.

PREFACE TO MUSIC.

THE slave music of the South presents a field for research and study very extensive and rich, and one, which has been scarcely more than entered upon.

There are evidently, I think, two legitimate methods of treating this music: either to render it in its absolute, rude simplicity, or to develop it without destroying its original characteristics; the only proper field for such development being in the harmony.

Practical experience shows the necessity, in some cases, in making compensation for its loss in being transplanted. Half its effectiveness, in its home, depends upon accompaniments, which can be carried away only in memory. The inspiration of numbers; the overpowering chorus, covering, defects; the swaying of the body; the rhythmical stamping of the feet; and all the wild enthusiasm of the negro camp-meeting--these evidently can not be transported to the boards of a public performance. To secure variety and do justice to the music, I have, therefore, treated it by both methods. The most characteristic of the songs are left entirely or nearly untouched. On the other hand, the improvement which a careful bringing out of the various parts has effected in such pieces as "*Some o' dese Mornin's*," "*Bright Sparkles in de Churchyard*," "*Dust an' Ashes*," and "*The Church ob God*," which seemed especially susceptible to such development, suggests possibilities of making more than has ever yet been made out of this slave music.

Another obstacle to its rendering is the fact that tones are frequently employed which we have no musical characters to represent. Such, for example, is that which I have indicated as nearly as possible by the flat seventh, in "*Great Camp-meetin'*," "*Hard Trials*," and others. These tones are variable in pitch, ranging through an entire interval on different occasions, according to the inspiration of the singer. They are rarely discordant, and often add a charm, to the performance. It is of course impossible to explain them in words, and to those who wish to sing them, the best advice is that most useful in learning to pronounce a foreign language: *Study all the rules you please; then-- go listen to a native.*

One reason for publishing this slave music is, that it is rapidly passing away. It may be that this people which has developed such a wonderful musical sense in its degradation will, in its maturity, produce a composer who could bring a music of the future out of this music of the past. At present, however, the freedmen have an unfortunate inclination to despise it, as a vestige of slavery; those who learned it in the old time, when it was the natural outpouring of their sorrows and longings, are dying off, and if efforts are not made for its preservation, the country will soon have lost this wonderful music of bondage.

THOMAS P. FENNER.

HAMPTON, VA., January 1, 1874.

CABIN AND PLANTATION SONGS.
Oh, den my little Soul's gwine to Shine.

"This was sung by a boy who was sold down South by his master; and when he parted from his mother, these were the words he sang."--J. H. BAILEY.

[1.
I'm gwine to jine de great 'sociation,
I'm gwine to jine de great 'sociation,
I'm gwine to jine de great 'sociation;

Hampton and Its Students

Den my little soul's gwine to shine, shine,
Den my little soul's gwine to shine along, Oh,]

2
I'm gwine to climb up Jacob's ladder, Den my little soul, &c.

3
I'm gwine to climb up higher and higher, Den my little soul, &c.

4
I'm gwine to sit down at the welcome table, Den my little soul, &c.

5
I'm gwine to feast off milk and honey, Den my little soul, &c.

6
I'm gwine to tell God how-a you sarved me, Den my little soul, &c.

7
I'm gwine to jine de big baptizin', Den my little soul, &c.

Peter, go Ring dem Bells.

"A secret prayer-meeting song, sung by Thomas Vess, a blacksmith and a slave. He especially sang it when any one confessed religion. Thomas Vess was a man whose heart was given to these songs, for in the neighborhood where he lived, it seemed like a prayer-meeting did not go on well without him. I have long since learned wherever he was known what happiness he got from them."

J. M. WADDY.

Peter, go Ring dem Bells.

"A secret prayer-meeting song, sung by Thomas Vess, a blacksmith and a slave. He especially sang it when any one confessed religion. Thomas Vess was a man whose heart was given to these songs, for in the neighborhood where he lived, it seemed like a prayer-meeting did not get on well without him. I have long since learned wherever he was known what happiness he got from them."
J. M. WADDY.

1. Oh Peter, go ring dem bells, Peter, go ring dem bells, Peter, go ring dem bells, I heard from heav-en to-day. I wonder where my mother is gone, I wonder where my mother is gone, I wonder where my mother is gone, I heard from heav-en to-day.

[1. Oh Peter, go ring dem bells,
Peter, go ring dem bells,
Peter, go ring dem bells,
I heard from heaven to-day.
I wonder where my mother is gone,
I wonder where my mother is gone,
I wonder where my mother is gone,
I heard from heaven to-day.
I heard from heaven to-day,
I heard from heaven to-day,
I thank God, and I thank you too,
I heard from heaven to-day.]

2
I wonder where sister Mary's gone--
I heard from heaven to-day;
I wonder where sister Martha's gone--
I heard from heaven to-day;
It's good news, and I thank God--

I heard from heaven to-day.
Oh, Peter, go ring dem bells--
I heard from heaven to-day.
CHO.--I heard from heaven, &c.

3
I wonder where brudder Moses gone--
I heard from heaven to-day;
I wonder where brudder Daniel's gone--
I heard from heaven to-day;
He's gone where Elijah has gone--
I heard from heaven to-day;
Oh, Peter, go ring dem bells--
I heard from heaven to-day.
CHO.--I heard from heaven, &c.

My Lord, what a Morning.

[1.
My Lord, what a morning,
My Lord, what a morning,
My Lord, what a morning,
When de stars begin to fall.
You'll hear de trumpet sound,

Hampton and Its Students

To wake de nations underground,
Look in my God's right hand,
When de stars begin to fall.
You'll hear de sinner moan,
To wake de nations underground,
Look in my God's right hand,
When de stars begin to fall.]

2
You'll hear de Christians shout, To wake, &c.
Look in my God's right hand, When de stars, &c.
You'll hear de angels sing, To wake, &c.
Look in my God's right hand, When de stars, &c.
CHO.--My Lord, what a morning, &c.

3
You'll see my Jesus come, To wake, &c.
Look in my God's right hand, When de stars, &c.
His chariot wheels roll round, To wake, &c.
Look in my God's right hand, When de stars, &c.
CHO.--My Lord, what a morning, &c.

Hail! Hail! Hail!

[Children, hail! hail! hail!
I'm gwine jine saints above;
Hail! hail! hail!
I'm on my journey home.
Oh, look up yander, what I see,
I'm on my journey home.
Bright angels comin' arter me,
I'm on my journey home.]

2
If you git dere before I do,
I'm on my journey home--

Look out for me--I'm comin' too;
I'm on my journey home.
CHO.--Children, hail, &c.

3
Oh, hallelujah to de Lamb!
I'm on my journey home;
King Jesus died for ebry man,
I'm on my journey home.
CHO.--Children, hail, &c.

Love an' serve de Lord.

[If ye love God, serve Him,
Hallelujah, Praise ye de Lord!
If ye love God, serve Him,
Hallelujah! Love an' serve de Lord.
Good mornin', brother trav'ler,
Pray tell me where you're bound?
I'm bound for Canaan's happy land,
And de enchanted ground.

CHO.--Come go to glory with me,
Come go to glory with me.]

2
Oh, when I was a sinner,
I liked my way so well;
But when I come to find out,
I was on de road to hell.
CHO.--I fleed to Jesus--Hallelujah! &c.
Oh, Jesus received me, Hallelujah, &c.

3
De Father, He looked on de Son, and smiled,
De Son, He looked on me;
De Father, redeemed my soul from hell;
An' de Son, He set me free.
CHO.--I shouted Hallelujah! Hallelujah, &c.
I praised my Jesus, Hallelujah, &c.

4
Oh when we all shall get dere,
Upon dat-a heavenly sho',
We'll walk about dem-a golden streets,
An' nebber part no mo'.
CHO--No rebukin' in de churches--Hallelujah,
Ebery day be Sunday--Hallelujah, &c.

Swing low, sweet Chariot.

[Oh swing low, sweet chariot,
Swing low, sweet chariot,
Swing low, sweet chariot,
I don't want to leave me behind.
Oh de good ole chariot swing so low,

Good ole chariot swing so low,
Oh de good ole chariot swing so low,
I don't want to leave me behind.]

2
Oh de good ole chariot will take us all home,
I don't want to leave me behind.
CHO.--Oh swing low, sweet chariot, &c.

My Bretheren, don't get Weary.

My Bretheren, don't get Weary.

[My bretheren, don't get weary,
Angels brought de tiding down;
Don't get weary,
I'm hunting for a home.
You'd better be a praying,
I do love de Lord;
For judgment day is a coming,
I do love de Lord.]

2
Oh whar you runnin', sinner?
I do love de Lord--
De judgment day is a comin'!
I do love de Lord.
CHO.--My bretheren, &c.

3
You'll see de world on fire!
I do love de Lord--
You'll see de element a meltin',
I do love de Lord.
CHO.--My bretheren, &c.

4
You'll see de moon a bleedin';
I do love de Lord--
You'll see the stars a fallin';
I do love de Lord.
CHO--My bretheren, &c.

Nobody knows de trouble I've Seen.

(This song was a favorite in the Sea Islands. Once when there had been a good deal of ill feeling excited, and trouble was apprehended, owing to the uncertain action of the Government in regard to the confiscated lands on the Sea Islands, Gen. Howard was called upon to address the colored people earnestly. To prepare them to listen, he asked them to sing. Immediately an old woman on the outskirts of the meeting began "Nobody knows the trouble I've seen," and the whole audience joined in. The General was so affected by the plaintive melody, that he found it difficult to maintain his official dignity.)

Nobody knows de trouble I've Seen.

1
[Oh, nobody knows de trouble I've seen,
Nobody knows but Jesus,
Nobody knows de trouble I've seen.
Glory Hallelujah!
Some-times I'm up, sometimes I'm down;
Oh, yes, Lord;
Sometimes I'm almost to de groun',
Oh, yes, Lord.
Although you see me goin' 'long so
Oh, yes, Lord;
I have my trials here below,
Oh, yes, Lord.]

2
One day when I was walkin' along,
Oh yes, Lord--
De element opened, an' de Love came down,
Oh yes, &c.
I never shall forget dat day,
Oh yes, &c.
When Jesus washed my sins away,
Oh yes, &c.
CHO.--Oh, nobody knows de trouble I've seen, &c.

View de Land

View de Land

[Oh way over Jerdan, View de land, View de land--
Way over Jerdan, Go view de heavenly land.
I'm born of God, I know I am; View de land, View de land;
And you deny it, if-a you can, Go view de heav'nly land.
I want to go to heaven when I die; View de land, View de land;
To shout salvation as-a I fly, Go view de heav'nly land.]

2
What kind o' shoes is dem-a you wear? View de land, &c.
Dat you can walk upon de air? Go view, &c.
Dem shoes I wear am de gospel shoes; View de land, &c.
An' you can wear dem ef-a you choose; Go view, &c.--*Cho.*

3
Der' is a tree in Paradise; View de land, &c.
De Christian he call it de tree ob life; Go view, &c.
I spects to eat de fruit right off o' dat tree; View de land, &c.,
Ef busy old Satan will let-a me be; Go view, &c.--*Cho.*

4
You say yer Jesus set-a you free; View de land, &c.
Why don't you let-a your neighbor be? Go view, &c.
You say you're aiming for de skies; View de land, &c.
Why don't you stop-a your telling lies; Go view, &c.--*Cho.*

The Danville Chariot.

The Danville Chariot.

[Oh swing low, sweet chariot, Pray let me enter in,
I don' want to stay here no longer.
I done been to heaven, an' I done been tried,
I been to de water, an' I been baptized,
I don' want to stay here no longer.
Oh down to de water I was led,
My soul got fed with de heav'nly bread
I don' want to stay here no longer.]

2
I had a little book, an' I read it through,
I got my Jesus as well as you;
I don' want to stay here no longer;
Oh I got a mother in de promised land,
I hope my mother will feed dem lambs;
I don' want to stay here no longer.
CHO.--Oh swing low, sweet chariot, &c.

3
Oh, some go to church for to holler an' shout,
Before six months dey're all turned out;
I don' want to stay here no longer.
Oh, some go to church for to laugh an' talk,
But dey knows nothin' bout dat Christian walk;
I don' want to stay here no longer.
CHO.--Oh, swing low, sweet chariot, &c.

4
Oh shout, shout, de deb'l is about;
Oh shut your do' an' keep him out;
I don' want to stay here no longer.
For he is so much-a like-a snaky in de grass,
Ef you don' mind he will get you at las',
I don' want to stay here no longer.
CHO.--Oh, swing low, sweet chariot, &c.

Ef ye want to see Jesus.

"My father sang this hymn, and said he knew a time when a great many slaves were allowed to have a revival for two days, while their masters and their families had one; and a great many professed religion. And one poor, ignorant man, professed religion, and praised God, and sang this hymn."

Ef ye want to see Jesus.

Ef ye want to see Jesus.—*Concluded.*

[Ef ye want to see Jesus, Go in de wilderness, Go in de wilderness, Go in de wilderness,
Ef ye want to see Jesus, Go in de wilderness, Leanin' on de Lord.
Oh, brother how d'ye feel, when ye come out de wilderness,
come out de wilderness, come out de wilderness.
Oh, brudder how d'ye feel, when ye come out de wilderness,
Leanin' on de Lord.
I felt so happy when I come out de wilderness,
come out de wilderness, oome out de wildorness.
I felt so happy when I come out de wilderness
Leaning on de Lerd.]
Oh, leanin' on de Lord, Leanin' on de Lord,
Oh leanin' upon de Lamb of God, who was slain on Calvary.]

2
I shouted Hallelujah, when I come out de wilderness--Leanin' on de Lord;
I heard de angels singin', when I come out de wilderness--Leanin' on de Lord;

I heard de harps a harpin,' when I come out de wilderness--Leanin' on de Lord.
CHO--Oh, leanin' on de Lord.

3
I heard de angels moanin', when I come out de wilderness--Leanin' on de Lord;
I heard de deb'l howlin', when I come out de wilderness--Leanin' on de Lord;
I gib de deb'l a battle, when I come out de wilderness--Leanin' on de Lord.
CHO.--Oh, leanin' on de Lord.

Oh, Yes.

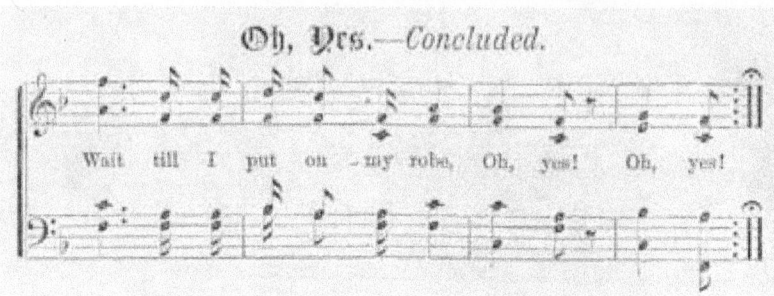

[Oh, yes! Oh, yes! I tell ye, bretheren, a mortal fac', Oh, yes! Oh, yes!
Ef ye want to get to heab'n, don't nebber look back, Oh, yes! Oh, yes!
I want to know-a before I go, Oh, yes! Oh, yes!
Yea, whether you love-a de Lord or no, Oh, yes! Oh, yes!
Ebber since I hab-a been newly born. Oh, yes! Oh, yes!
I love for to see-a God's work go on,
Oh, wait till I put on my robe, wait till I put on my robe,
Wait till I put on my robe, Oh, yes! Oh, Yes!]

2.
Ef eber I land on de oder sho', Oh, yes,
I'll nebber come here for to sing no mo', Oh, yes;
A golden band all round my waist,
An' de palms ob vic-a-try in-a my hand,
An' de golden slippers on to my feet,
Gwine to walk up an' down o' dem golden street.
CHO.--Oh, wait till I put on my robe.

3.
An' my lovely bretherin, dat aint all, Oh, yes,
I'm not done a talkin' about my Lord;
An' a golden crown a-placed on a-my head,
An' my long white robe, a-come-a-dazzlin' down,
Now wait till I get on my gospel shoes,
Gwine to walk about de heaben an' a-carry de news.
CHO.--Oh, wait till I put on my robe.

4.
I'm anchored in Christ, Christ anchored in me, Oh, yes, &c.,

All de deb'ls in hell can't-a-pluck a-me out;
An' I wonder what Satan 's grumbulin' about,
He's bound into hell, an' he can't git out.
But he shall be loose an' hab his sway,
Yea at de great resurrection day.
CHO.--Oh, wait till I put on my robe.

Verses, some of which are often added as encores.

5.
I went down de hill side to make a-one prayer, Oh, yes,
An' when I got dere, old Satan was dere, Oh, yes,
An' what do ye t'ink he said to me? Oh, yes,
Said, "Off from here you'd better be." Oh, yes;
An' what for to do, I did not know, Oh, yes,
But I fell on my knees, an' I cried, Oh, Lord, Oh, yes,
Now my Jesus bein' so good an' kind,
Yea, to de with-er-ed, halt an' blind;
My Jesus lowered his mercy down,
An' snatch-a-me from a-dem doors ob hell,
He snatch-a-me from dem doors ob hell,
An' took-a me in a-wid him to dwell.
CHO.--Oh, wait, till I put on my robe.

6.
I was in de church an' prayin' loud,
An' on my knees to my Jesus bowed,
Ole Satan tole me to my face,
"I'll git you when-a-you leave dis place;"
Oh, brother, dat scare me to my heart,
I was 'fraid to walk a-when it was dark.
CHO.--Oh, wait till I get on my robe.

7.
I started home, but I did pray,
An' I met Ole Satan on de way;
Ole Satan made a-one grab at me,
But he missed my soul, an' I went free.
My sins went a-lumberin, down to hell,
An' my soul went a-leapin' up Zion's hill;

Hampton and Its Students

I tell ye what, bretherin, you'd better not laugh,
Ole Satan 'll run you down his path;
If he runs you, as he run me,
You'll be glad to fall upon your knee.
CHO.--Oh, wait till I put on my robe.

Run, Mary, Run.

[Run, Mary, run, Run, Mary, run, Oh, Run, Mary, run,
I know de oder worl' 'm not like dis.
Fire in de east, an' fire in de west,
I know de oder worl' 'm not like dis,
Bound to burn de wilderness,
I know de oder worl' 'm not like dis.
Jordan's riber is a riber to cross,
I know de oder worl' 'm not like dis,
Stretch your rod an' come across, I know, &c.]

2
Swing low, chariot, into de east, I know, &c.

Let God's children hab some peace; I know, &c.
Swing low, chariot, into de west; I know, &c.

Let God's children hab some rest; I know, &c.--CHO.

3
Swing low, chariot, into de north; I know, &c.
Gib me de gold widout de dross; I know, &c.
Swing low, chariot, into de south; I know, &c.
Let God's children sing and shout; I know, &c.--CHO.

4
Ef dis day war judgment day, I know, &c.
Ebery sinner would want to pray; I know, &c.
Dat trouble it come like a gloomy cloud; I know, &c.
Gader tick, an' tunder loud; I know, &c.--CHO.

Religion is a Fortune.

Religion is a Fortune.

[Oh, religion is a fortune, I raly do believe,
Oh, religion is a fortune, I raly do believe,
Oh, religion is a fortune, I raly do believe,
Whar sabbaths have no end.
Whar ye been, poor mourner, whar ye been so long;
Been low down in de valley for to pray,
An' I aint done praying yet.]

2
Gwine to sit down in de kingdom, I raly do believe,
Whar Sabbaths, &c.,
Gwine to walk about in Zion, I raly do believe,

Whar Sabbaths, &c.
Duo.--Whar ye ben young convert, &c.

3
Gwine to see my sister Mary, I raly do believe,
Whar Sabbaths, &c.
Gwine to see my brudder Jonah, I raly do believe.
Duo.--Whar ye ben good Christian, &c.

4
Gwine to talk-a wid de angels, I raly do believe,
Whar Sabbaths, &c.,
Gwine to see my massa Jesus, I raly do believe,
Whar Sabbaths, &c.

Some o' dese Mornin's.

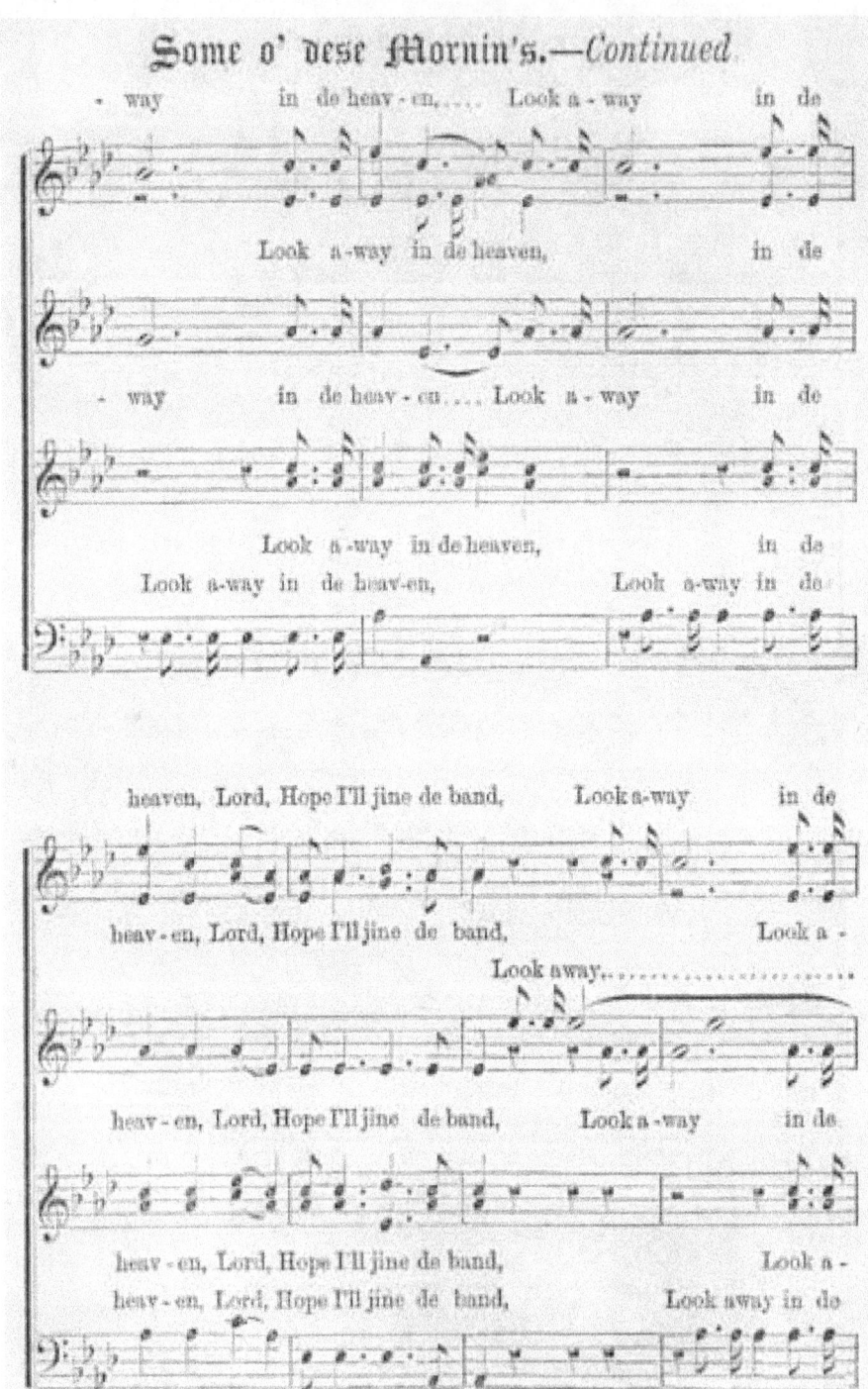

[Gwine to see my mother some o' dese mornin's,
see my mother some o' dese mornin's,
See my mother, some o' dese mornin's,
Hope I'll jine de band.
Oh, sittin' in de kingdom some o' dese mornin's,
sittin' in de kingdom some o' dese mornin's,
Sittin' in de kingdom, some o' dese mornin's,
Hope I'll jine de band.
Look away in de heaven,
Look away in de heaven,
Look away in de heaven,
Lord, Hope I'll jine de band,
Look away in de heaven,
Look away in de heaven,
Look away in de heaven,
Lord, Hope I'll jine de band,]

2
Gwine to see my brother some o' dese mornin's;
Oh, shouting in de heaven some o' dese mornin's,
Hope I'll jine de band.
CHO.--Look away.

3
Gwine to walk about in Zion, some o' dese mornin's,
Gwine to talk-a with de angels some o' dese mornin's,
Hope I'll jine de band.
CHO.--Look away.

4
Gwine to talk de trouble ober some o' dese mornin's,
Gwine to see my Jesus some o' dese mornin's,
Hope I'll jine de band.
CHO.--Look away.

Page 193

My Lord delibered Daniel.

[My Lord delibered Daniel,
My Lord delibered Daniel,
My Lord delibered Daniel;
Why can't he deliber me?
I met a pilgrim on de way,
An' I ask him whar he's a gwine.
I'm bound for Canaan's happy lan',
An' dis is de shouting band. Go on!]

2.
Some say dat John de Baptist
Was nothing but a Jew,
But de Bible doth inform us

Dat he was a preacher, too;
Yes, he was!
CHO.--My Lord delibered Daniel.

3.
Oh, Daniel cast in de lions den,
He pray both night an' day,
De angel came from Galilee,
An' lock de lions' jaw.
Dat's so.
CHO.--My Lord delibered Daniel.

4.
He delibered Daniel from de lions' den,
Jonah from de belly ob de whale,
And de Hebrew children from de fiery furnace,
And why not ebery man?
Oh, yes!
CHO.--My Lord delibered Daniel.

5.
De richest man dat eber I saw
Was de one dat beg de most,
His soul was filled wid Jesus,
And wid de Holy Ghost.
Yes it was!
CHO.--My Lord delibered Daniel.

Oh, wasn't dat a wide Riber.

[Oh, wasn't dat a wide riber,
Riber ob Jordan, Lord, Wide riber,
Dere's one more riber to cross;
Oh, you got Jesus, hold him fast.
One more riber to cross,
Oh, better love was nebber told,
One more riber to cross.
'Tis stronger dan an iron band,
One more riber to cross,
'Tis sweeter dan dat honey comb,
One more riber to cross.]

2.
Oh, de good ole chariot passing by,
One more riber to cross,
She jarred de earth an' shook de sky,
One more, &c.,
I pray, good Lord, shall I be one?
One more, &c.,
To get up in de chariot, trabbel on,
One more, &c.
CHO.--Oh, wasn't dat a wide riber? &c.

3.
We're told dat de fore-wheel run by love,
One more, &c.,
We're told dat de hind wheel run by faith,
One more, &c.,
I hope I shall get dere bimeby,
One more, &c.,
To jine de number in de sky,
One more, &c.
CHO.--Oh, wasn't dat a wide riber? &c.

4.
Oh, one more riber we hab to cross,
One more, &c.,
'Tis Jordan's riber we hab to cross,
One more, &c.,

Oh, Jordan's riber am chilly an' cold,
One more, &c.,
But I got de glory in-a my soul,
One more. &c.
CHO.--Oh, wasn't dat a wide riber? &c.

Oh, give way, Jordan.

[Oh, give way, Jordan, give way, Jordan,
Oh, give way, Jordan, I want to go across to see my Lord.
Oh, I heard a sweet music up above,
I want to go across to see my Lord;
An' I wish dat music would come here,
I want to go across to see my Lord.
Oh, I heard a sweet music in de air,
I want to go across to see my Lord;
An' I wish dat music would come here,
I want to go across to see my Lord.]

2.
Oh, stow back, stow back de powers of hell,
I want to go across to see my Lord,
And let God's children take de field,
I want to go across to see my Lord.
Now stan' back Satan, let me go by,
I want to go across, &c.,
Gwine to serve my Jesus till I die,
I want to go across, &c.--CHO.

3.
Soon in de mornin' by de break ob day
I want to go across, &c.,
See de ole ship ob Zion sailin' away,
I want to go across, &c.,
Now I must go across, an' I shall go across,
I want to go across, &c.,
Dis sinful world I count but dross,
I want to go across, &c.--CHO.

4.
Oh, I heard such a lumbering in de sky,
I want to go across, &c.,
It make a-me t'ink my time was nigh,
I want to go across, &c.,
Yes, it must be my Jesus in de cloud,
I want to go across, &c.,

Hampton and Its Students

I nebber heard him speak so loud--
I want to go across, &c.--CHO.

John Saw.

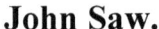

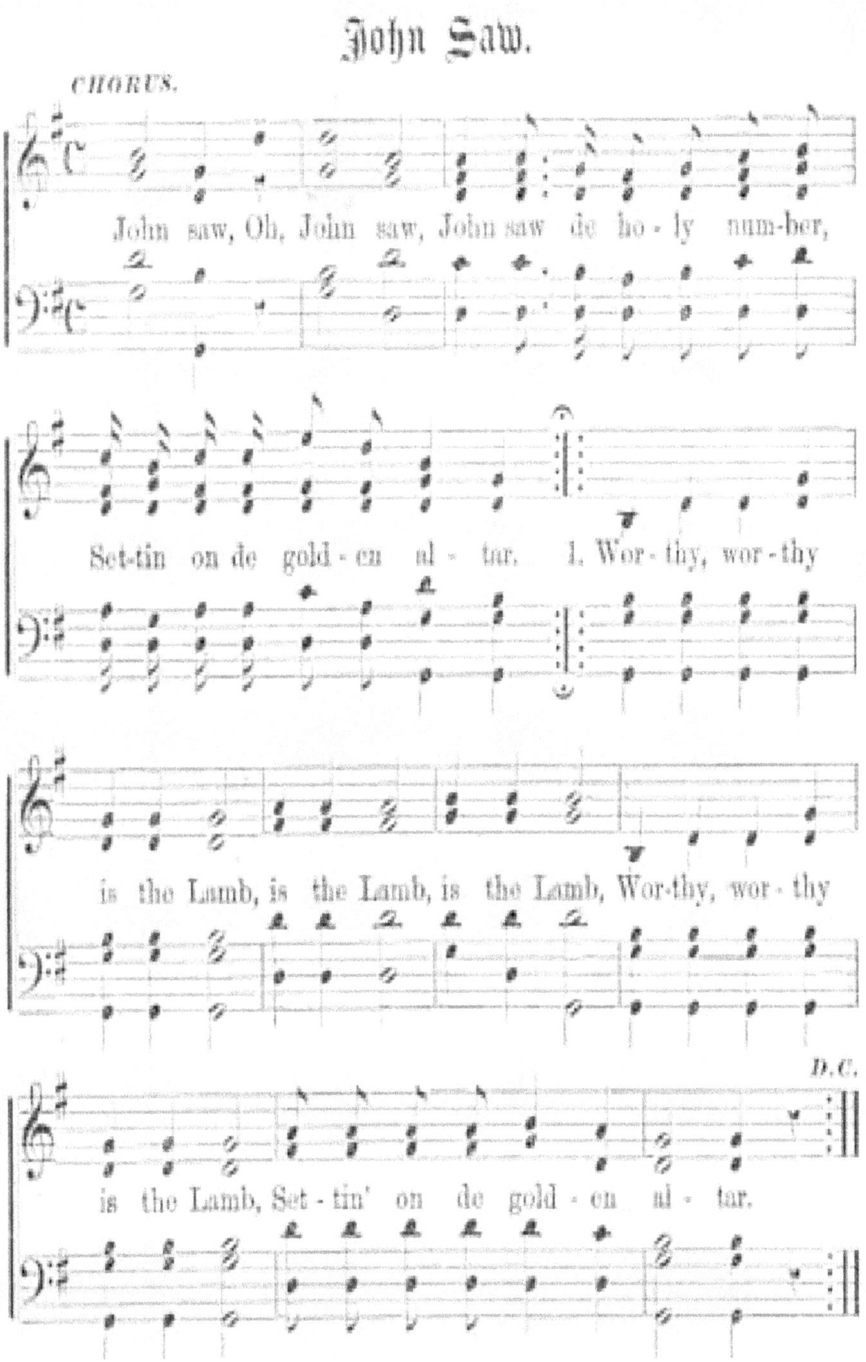
John Saw.
CHORUS.
John saw, Oh, John saw, John saw de ho - ly num-ber,
Set-tin on de gold - en al - tar. 1. Wor - thy, wor - thy
is the Lamb, is the Lamb, is the Lamb, Wor-thy, wor - thy
D.C.
is the Lamb, Set - tin' on de gold - en al - tar.

[John saw, Oh, John saw, John saw de holy number,
Settin on de golden altar.
1.
Worthy, worthy is the Lamb, is the Lamb, is the Lamb,
Worthy, worthy is the Lamb, Settin' on de golden altar.]

2
Mary wept, an' Martha cried--Settin' on, &c.
To see de'r Saviour crucified--Settin' on, &c.
Weepin' Mary, weep no more--Settin' on, &c.
Jesus say He gone before--Settin' on, &c.
CHO.--John saw, &c.

3
Want to go to hebben when I die--Settin' on, &c.
Shout salvation as I fly--Settin' on, &c.
It's a little while longer here below--Settin' on, &c.
Den-a home to glory we shall go--Settin' on, &c.
CHO.--John saw, &c.

King Emanuel.

[1. Oh, who do you call de King Emanuel;
I call my Jesus King Emanuel.
Oh de King Emanuel is a mighty 'manuel;
I call my Jesus King Emanuel.]

2
Oh, some call Him Jesus; but I call Him Lord,
I call my Jesus King Emanuel;
Let's talk about de hebben, an' de hebben's fine t'ings,
I call my Jesus King Emanuel.
CHO.--Oh de King Emanuel, &c.

3
Oh steady, steady, a little while;
I call my Jesus King Emanuel;
I will tell you what my Lord done for me;

I call my Jesus King Emanuel.
CHO.--Oh de King Emanuel, &c.

4
He pluck-a my feet out de miry clay;
I call my Jesus King Emanuel;
He sot dem a-on de firm Rock o' Age;
I call my Jesus King Emanuel.
CHO.--Oh de King Emanuel, &c.

De ole Sheep done know de Road.

[Oh de ole sheep done know de road,
De ole sheep done know de road,
De ole sheep done know de road,
De young lambs mus' find de way.
Oh, sooner in de mornin' when I rise,
De young lambs mus' find de way.
Wid crosses an' trials on ebry side,
De young lambs must find de way.
My brudder aint ye got yer counts all sealed,
De young lambs, &c.
You'd better go get em 'fore ye leave dis field,
De young lambs, &c.]

2
Oh, shout my sister, for you are free, De young lambs, &c.,
For Christ hab bought your liberty, De young lambs, &c.,
I raly do believe widout one doubt, De young lambs, &c.,
Dat de Christian hab a mighty right to shout, De young lambs, &c.
CHO.--Oh, de ole sheep, &c.

3
My brudder, better mind how you walk on de cross, De young lambs, &c.,
For your foot might slip, an' yer soul git lost, De young lambs, &c.,
Better mind dat sun, and see how she run, De young lambs, &c.,
An' mind don't let her catch ye wid yer works undone, De young lambs, &c.
CHO.--Oh, de ole sheep, &c.

De Church of God.

[De church of God dat sound so sweet,
De church, de church of God
Oh, look up yander what I see
Bright angels comin' arter me.]

2.
Oh, Jesus tole you once before,
To go in peace an' sin no more;
Oh, Paul an' Silas bound in jail,
Den one did sing, an' de oder pray.
CHO.--De church ob God, &c.

3.
Oh, did you hear my Jesus say
"Come unto me, I am de way;"
Oh, come along, Moses, don't get lost,
Oh, stretch your rod, an' come across.
CHO--De church ob God, &c.

Bright Sparkles in de Churchyard.

This peculiar but beautiful medley was a great favorite among the hands in the tobacco factories in Danville, Va.

Hampton and Its Students

[May de Lord--He *will* be glad of me
May de Lord--He *will* be glad of me
May de Lord--He *will* be glad of me;
In de heaven He'll rejoice.
In de heaven, once, In de heaven, twice,
In de heaven He'll rejoice,
In de heaven, once, In de heaven, twice,
In de heaven He'll rejoice.]

[Bright sparkles in de churchyard,
Give light unto de tomb,
Bright summer, spring's over,
Sweet flowers in de'r bloom.
Bright sparkles in de church-yard,
Give light unto de tomb,
Bright summer, spring's over,
Sweet flowers in de'r bloom.
My mother, once, my mother, twice,
my mother she'll rejoice.

In de heaven, once, in de heaven, twice,
In de heaven she'll rejoice.
Mother, rock me in de cradle all de day
Mother, rock me in de cradle all de day
Mother, rock me in de cradle all de day
Mother, rock me in de cradle all de day,

All de day, all de day
Oh, rock me in de cradle all de day,
all de day, all de day,
Oh, rock me in de cradle all de day.
Oh, mother, don't ye love yer darlin' child,
Oh, rock me in de cradle all de day

Oh, mother, don't ye love yer darlin' child?
Oh, rock me in de cradle all de day
Mother, rock me in de cradle,
rock me in de cradle,
rock me in de cradle all de day

Hampton and Its Students

All de day, all de day
Oh, rock me in de cradle all de day,

all de day, all de day,
Oh, rock me in de cradle all de day.
You may lay me down to sleep, my mother dear,
Oh, rock me in de cradle all de day,
You may lay me down to sleep, my mother dear,
Oh, rock me in de cradle all de day,]

Judgment Day is a-rollin' around.

Judgment Day is a-rollin' around.—*Concluded*.

[Judgment, Judgment, Judgment day is a-rollin' around,
Judgment, Judgment, Oh, how I long to go.
I've a good ole mudder in de heaven, my Lord,
Oh, how I long to go dere too;
I've a good ole mudder in de heaven, my Lord,
Oh, how I long to go.
I've a good ole fader in de heaven, my Lord,
Oh, how I long to go dere too;.
I've a good ole fader in de heaven, my Lord,
Oh, how I long to go.
Judgment, Judgment, Judgment day is a-rollin' around,
Judgment, Judgment, Oh, how I long to go.

2.
Dar's a long white robe in de heaven for me,
Oh, how I long to go dere too;
Dar's a starry crown in de heaven for me,
Oh, how I long to go.
My name is written in de book ob life,
Oh, how I long to go dere too,
Ef you look in de book you'll fin'em dar,
Oh, how I long to go.

3.
Brudder Moses gone to de kingdom, Lord,

Oh, how I long to go dere too;
Sister Mary gone to de kingdom, Lord,
Oh, how I long to go.
Dar's no more slave in de kingdom, Lord,
Oh, how I long to go dere too,
All is glory in de kingdom, Lord,
Oh, how I long to go.

4.
My brudder build a house in Paradise,
Oh, how I long to go dere too;
He built it by dat ribber of life,
Oh, how I long to go.
Dar's a big camp meetin' in de kingdom, Lord,
Oh, how I long to go dere too,
Come, let us jine dat a heavenly crew,
Oh, how I long to go.

5.
King Jesus sittin' in de kingdom, Lord,
Oh, how I long to go dere too;
De angels singin' all round de trone,
Oh, how I long to go.
De trumpet sound de Jubilo,
Oh, how I long to go dere too,
I hope dat trump will blow me home,
Oh, how I long to go.]

Oh, Sinner, you'd better get ready.

Oh, Sinner, you'd better get ready.—Concluded.

[Oh, sinner, you'd better get ready,
Ready, my Lord, ready,
Oh, sinner, you'd better get ready,
For the time is a-comin' dat sinner must die.
Oh, sinner man, you had better pray,
Time is a-comin' dat sinner must die;
For it look-a like judgment ebry day.
Time is a-comin' dat sinner must die;
I heard a lumbring in de sky,
Time is a-comin' dat sinner must die,
Dat make-a me t'ink my time was nigh,
Time is a-com-in' dat sinner must die.

2.
I heard of my Jesus a many one say--
Time is a-comin' dat sinner must die,
Could 'move poor sinner's sins away--
Time is a-comin' dat sinner must die.
Yes, I'd rather a pray myself away--
Time is a-comin' dat sinner must die,

Dan to lie in hell an' burn a-one day--
Time is a-comin' dat sinner must die.
CHO.--Oh, sinner, you'd better get ready, &c.

3.
I think I heard a my mother say--
Time is a-comin' dat sinner must die,
'Twas a pretty thing a to serve de Lord--
Time is a-comin' dat sinner must die.
Oh, when I get to Heaven I'll be able for to tell--
Time is a-comin' dat sinner must die,
Oh, how I shun dat dismal hell--
Time is a-comin' dat sinner must die.
CHO.--Oh, sinner, you'd better get ready, &c.

Hear de Lambs a Cryin'.

[You hear de lambs a cryin',
Hear de lambs a cryin',
Hear de lambs a cryin',
Oh, shepherd, feed-a my sheep.
Our Saviour spoke dese words so sweet:
"Oh shepherd, feed a my sheep,"
Said, "Peter, if ye love me, feed my sheep."
Oh, shepherd, feed-a my sheep.
Oh, Lord, I love Thee, Thou dost know;
Oh, shepherd, feed a my sheep;
Oh, give me grace to love Thee mo';
Oh, shepherd, feed a my sheep.

2
I don' know what you want to stay here for, Oh, shepherd, &c.,
For dis vain world's no friend to grace, Oh, shepherd, &c.,
If I only had wings like Noah's dove, Oh, shepherd, &c.,
I'd fly away to de heavens above, Oh, shepherd, &c.
CHO.--You hear de lambs crying, &c.

3
When I am in an agony, Oh, shepherd, &c.,
When you see me, pity me, Oh, shepherd, &c.,
For I am a pilgrim travellin' on, Oh, shepherd, &c.,
De lonesome road where Jesus gone, Oh, shepherd, &c.
CHO.--You hear de lambs a-crying, &c.

4
Oh, see my Jesus hanging high, Oh, shepherd. &c.,
He looked so pale an' bled so free, Oh, shepherd, &c.,
Oh, don't you think it was a shame, Oh, shepherd, &c.,
He hung three hours in dreadful pain, Oh, shepherd, &c.
CHO.--You hear de lambs a-crying, &c.

Rise and Shine.

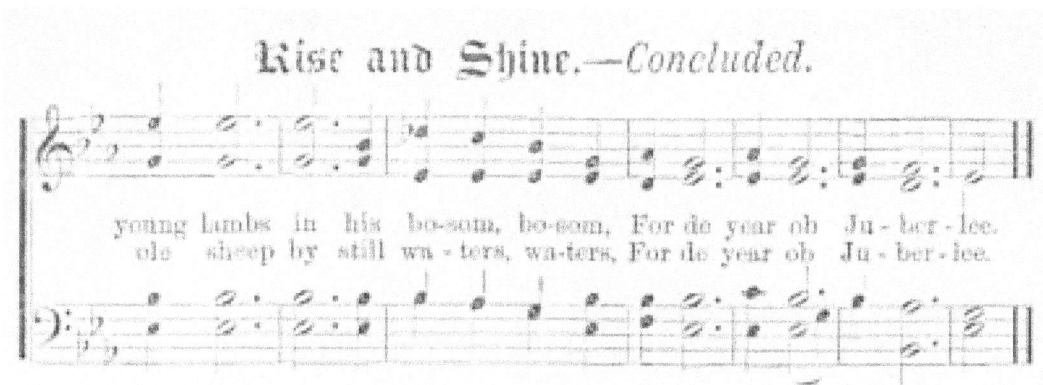

[Oh, rise an' shine, an' give God de glory, glory,
Rise an' shine, an' give God de glory, glory,
Rise an' shine, an' give God de glory, glory, for de year of Juberlee.

1
Jesus carry de young lambs in his bosom, bosom,
Carry de young lambs in his bosom, bosom,
Carry de young lambs in his bosom, bosom,
For de year ob Juberlee.
Jesus lead de ole sheep by still waters, waters,
Lead de ole sheep by still waters, waters,
Lead de ole sheep by still waters, waters,
For de year ob Juberlee.

2
Oh, come on, mourners, get you ready, ready,
Come on, mourners, get you ready, ready, (*bis*),
For de year ob jubilee;
You may keep your lamps trimmed an' burning, burning,
Keep your lamps trimmed an' burning, burning, (*bis*),
For de year ob jubilee.
CHO.--Oh, rise an' shine, &c.

3
Oh, come on, children, don't be weary, weary,
Come on, children, don't be weary, weary, (*bis*),
For de year ob jubilee;
Oh, don't you hear dem bells a-ringin', ringin',

Don't you hear dem bells a-ringin', ringin", (*bis*),
For de year ob jubilee.
CHO.--Oh, rise an' shine, &c.

Hard Trials.

De fox hab hole in de groun', An' de bird hab nest in de air,
An' eb-ry t'ing hab a hid-ing-place, But we, poor sin-ner, hab none.

CHORUS.
Now aint dat hard tri-als, great trib-u-la-tion, Aint dat hard

Hampton and Its Students

[De fox hab hole in de groun',
An' de bird hab nest in de air,
An' ebry t'ing hab a hiding-place,
But we, poor sinner, hab none.
Now aint dat hard trials, great tribulation,
Aint dat hard trials I'm boun' to leabe dis world.
1.
Baptist, Baptist is my name,
Baptist till I die, I'll be baptize in de Baptist name,
An' I'll lib on de Baptist side.

2.
Methodist, Methodist is my name,
Methodist till I die, I'll be baptize in de Methodist name,
An' I'll lib on de Methodist side.

3.
Presbyterian, Presbyterian, &c.
Presbyterian till, &c. Presbyterian name, &c.
lib on de Presbyterian side.

4.
You may go dis-a way,
You may go dat-a way,
You may go from do' to do',
But ef you habn't got de grace ob God in you heart,
De debil will get you sho'.

5.
Now while we are marchin' along dis dreadful road,
You had better stop your different names, An'--]

Most Done Trabelling.

[Oh, my mudder's in de road,
Most done trabelling;
My mudder's in de road,
Most done trabelling,
My mudder's in de road,
Most done trabelling.
I'm bound to carry my soul to de Lord.

I'm bound to carry my soul to my Jesus,
I'm bound to carry my soul to de Lord;]

2.
Oh, my sister's in de road,
Most done trabelling,
My sister's in de road, (*bis*)
Most done trabelling. (*bis*)
CHO.--I'm bound to carry, &c.

3.
Oh, my brudder's in de road,
Most done trabelling,
My brudder's in de road, (*bis*)
Most done trabelling. (*bis*)
CHO,--I'm bound to carry, &c.

4.
Oh, de preacher's in de road,
Most done trabelling,
De preacher's in de road, (*bis*)
Most done trabelling. (*bis*)
CHO.--I'm bound to carry, &c.

5.
All de member's in de road,
Most done trabelling,
De members' in de road, (*bis*)
Most done trabelling. (*bis*)
CHO.--I'm bound to carry, &c.

Gwine up.

Hampton and Its Students

[Oh, yes, I'm gwine up, gwine up, gwine all de way, Lord,
Gwine up, gwine up to see de hebbenly land,
Oh, yes, I'm gwine up, gwine up, gwine all de way, Lord,
Gwine up, gwine up to see de hebbenly land.
Oh, saints an' sinners will-a you go,
see de hebbenly land,
I'm a gwine up to heaven for to see my robe,
See de hebbenly land,
Gwine to see my robe an' try it on,
See de hebbenly land,
It's brighter dan-a dat glitterin' sun,
See de hebbenly land.]

2.
I'm a gwine to keep a climbin' high--
See de hebbenly land;
Till I meet dem-er angels in-a de sky--
See de hebbenly lan'.
Dem pooty angels I shall see--
See de hebbenly lan';
Why don't de debbil let-a me be--
See de hebbenly lan'.
CHO.--Oh yes, I'm gwine up, &c.

3.
I tell you what I like-a de best--
See de hebbenly lan';
It is dem-a shoutin' Methodess--
See de, hebbenly lan';
We shout so loud de debbil look--
See de hebbenly lan';
An' he gets away wid his cluvven foot--
See de hebbenly lan'.
CHO.--Oh, yes, I'm gwine up, &c.

I hope my Mother will be there.

This was sung by the hands in Mayo's Tobacco Factory, Richmond, and is really called "The Mayo Boys' Song."

[I hope my mother will be there,
In that beautiful world on high.
That used to join with me in pray'r,
In that beautiful world on high.
Oh I will be there
Oh I will be there
With the palms of victory,
crowns of glory you shall wear
In that beautiful world on high.]

2
I hope my sister will be there,
In that beautiful world on high,
That used to join with me in prayer,
In that beautiful world on high.
CHO.--Oh, I will be there, &c.

3
I hope my brother will be there,
In that beautiful world on high,
That used to join with me in prayer,
In that beautiful world on high.
CHO.--Oh, I will be there, &c.

4
I know my Saviour will be there,
In that beautiful world on high,
That used to listen to my prayer,
In that beautiful world on high.
CHO.--Oh, I will be there, &c.

Oh, de Hebben is Shinin'.

[Oh de hebben is shinin', shinin',

O Lord, de hebben is shinin' full ob love.
Oh, Fare-you-well, friends, I'm gwine to tell you all;
De hebben is shinin' full ob love;
Gwine to leave you all a-mine eyes to close;
De hebben is shinin' full ob love.
Oh, when I build a my tent agin',
De hebben is shinin' full ob love;
Build it so ole Satan he can't get in;
De hebben, &c.]

2 Death say, "I come on a-dat hebbenly 'cree;
De hebben is, &c.
My warrant's for to summage thee;
De hebben is, &c.
An' whedder thou prepared or no;
De hebben is, &c.
Dis very day He say you must go;"
De hebben is, &c.--*Cho*.

3
Oh, ghastly Death, wouldst thou prevail;
De hebben is, &c.
Oh, spare me yet anoder day;
De hebben is, &c.
I'm but a flower in my bloom;
De hebben is, &c.
Why wilt thou cut-a me down so soon?
De hebben is, &c.--*Cho*.

4
Oh, if I had-a my time agin;
De hebben is, &c.
I would hate dat road-a dat leads to sin;
De hebben is, &c.
An' to my God a-wid earnest pray;
De hebben is, &c.
An' wrastle until de break o' day;
De hebben is, &c.--*Cho*.

Who'll jine de Union.

[Oh, Hallelujah, Oh, Hallelujah, Oh, Hallelujah, Lord,
Who'll jine de Union?
My lovely bretheren, how ye do?
Who'll jine de Union?
Oh, does yer love a-continue true?
Who'll jine de Union?
Eber since I hab-a-been newly born.
Who'll jine de Union?
I love for to see-a God's work go on,
Who'll jine de Union?

2.
Ef ye want to ketch-a dat hebbenly breeze,
Who'll jine de Union?
Go down in de valley upon yer knees,
Who'll jine de Union?
Go bend yer knees right smoove wid de groun',
Who'll jine de Union?
An' pray to de Lord to turn you roun',
Who'll jine de Union?
CHO.--Oh, Hallelujah, &c.

4.
Say, ef you belong to de Union ban',
Who'll jine de Union?
Den here's my heart, an' here's my han',
Who'll jine de Union?
I love yer all, both bond an' free,
Who'll jine de Union?
I love you ef-a you don't love me,

Hampton and Its Students

Who'll jine de Union?
CHO.--Oh, Hallelujah, &c.

3.
Now ef you want to know ob me,
Who'll jine de Union?
Jess who I am, an' a-who I be,
Who'll jine de Union?
I'm a chile ob God, wid my soul sot free,
Who'll jine de Union?
For Christ hab bought my liberty,
Who'll jine de Union?
CHO.--Oh, Hallelujah, &c.

A great Camp-meetin' in de Promised Land.

"This hymn was made by a company of Slaves, who were not allowed to sing or pray anywhere the old master could hear them; and when he died their old mistress looked on them with pity, and granted them the privilege of singing and praying in the cabins at night. Then they sang this hymn, and shouted for joy, and gave God the honor and praise."

J. B. TOWE.

[Oh walk togedder, childron, Dont yer get weary,
Walk togedder, childron, Dont yer get weary,
Walk togedder, childron,
Oh talk togedder, childron, Dont yer get weary,
Talk togedder, childron, Dont yer get weary,
Talk togedder, childron,
Oh sing togedder, childron, Dont yer get weary,
Sing togedder, childron, Dont yer get weary,
Sing togedder, childron,
Dont yer get weary,
Dere's a great camp-meetin' in de Promised Land.
Gwine to mourn an' nebber
Oh walk togedder, childron, Dont yer get weary,
Walk togedder, childron, Dont yer get weary,
Walk togedder, childron,
Oh talk togedder, childron, Dont yer get weary,
Talk togedder, childron, Dont yer get weary,
Talk togedder, childron,
Oh sing togedder, childron, Dont yer get weary,
Sing togedder, childron, Dont yer get weary,
Sing togedder, childron,

Dont yer get weary,
Dere's a great camp-meetin' in de Promised Land.
Gwine to mourn an' nebber tire, Mourn an' nebber tire,'
Mourn an' nebber tire,
Dere's a great camp-meetin' in de Promised Land.]

2.
Oh get you ready, children, Dont you get weary,
Get you ready, children, Dont you, &c.(*bis*.)
Dere's a great camp-meetin' in de Promised Land.
For Jesus is a comin', Dont you get, &c.,
Jesus is a comin', Dont you get, &c., (*bis*.)
Dere's a great camp-meetin' in de Promised Land.
Gwine to hab a happy meetin', Dont you get weary,
Hab a happy meetin', Dont you get, &c. (*bis*.)
Dere's a great camp-meetin' in de Promised Land.
CHO.--Gwine to pray an' nebber tire,
Pray an' nebber tire, (*bis*.)
Dere's a great camp-meetin' in de Promised Land.

3.
Gwine to hab it in hebben, Dont you, &c.
Gwine to hab it in hebben, Dont, &c. (*bis*.)
Dere's a great camp-meetin' in de, &c.,
Gwine to shout in hebben, Dont you get weary,
Shout in hebben, Dont you get, &c., (*bis*.)
Dere's a great camp-meetin' in de, &c.,
Oh will you go wid me, Dont you get, &c.,
Will you go wid me, Dont you get, &c., (*bis*.)
Dere's a great camp-meetin' in de, &c.,
CHO.--Gwine to shout an' nebber tire,
Shout an' nebber tire, (*bis*.)
Dere's a great camp-meetin' in de Promised Land,

4.
Dere's a better day comin', Dont you get weary,
Better day a comin', Dont you get, &c., (*bis*.)
Dere's a great camp-meetin' in de Promised Land.
Oh slap your hands children, Dont, &c.
Slap your hands children, Dont, &c., (*bis*.)

Dere's a great camp-meetin' in de Promised Land.
Oh pat your foot childron, Dont you get weary,
Pat your foot childron, Dont, &c., (*bis*.)
Dere's a great camp-meetin' in de Promised Land.
CHO.--Gwine to live wid God forever,
Live wid God forever, (*bis*.)
Dere's a great camp-meetin' in de Promised Land.

5.
Oh, feel de Spirit a movin', Dont you, &c.
Feel de Spirit a movin', Dont, &c., (*bis*.)
Dere's a great camp-meetin' in de, &c.
Oh now I'm gettin' happy, Dont you get weary,
Now I'm gettin' happy, Dont, &c., (*bis*.)
Dere's a great camp-meetin' in de, &c.
I feel so happy, Dont you get weary,
Feel so happy, Dont you get weary, (*bis*.)
Dere's a great camp-meetin' in de, &c.
CHO.--Oh, fly an' nebber tire,
Fly an' nebber tire, (*bis*.)
Dere's a great camp-meetin' in de Promised Land.

Good news, de Chariot's comin'.

[Good news, de chariot's comin',
good news, de chariot's comin',
good news, de chariot's comin',
I don' want her leave a me behind.
Gwine to get up in de chariot, Carry me home,
Get up in de chariot, Carry me home;
Get up in de chariot, Carry me home;
An' I don' want her leave a me behind.]

2
Dar's a long white robe in de hebben I know,
A long white robe in de hebben, I know,
A long white robe in de hebben, I know,
An' I don' want her leave-a me behind.
Dar's a golden crown in de hebben, I know,
A golden crown in de hebben, I know,

A golden crown in de hebben, I know,
An' I don' want her leave-a me behind.
CHO.--Good news, de chariot's comin', &c.

3
Dar's a golden harp in de hebben, I know,
A golden harp in de hebben, I know,
A golden harp in de hebben, I know,
An' I don' want her leave-a me behind.
Dar's silver slippers in de hebben, I know,
Silver slippers in de hebben, I know,
Silver slippers in de hebben, I know,
An' I don' want her leave-a me behind.
CHO.--Good news, de chariot's comin', &c.

Don't ye view dat ship a come a sailin'.

Dont ye view dat ship.—*Concluded.*

[Dont ye view dat ship a come a sailin'? Hallelujah,
Dont ye view dat ship a come a sailin'?
Dont ye view dat ship a come a sailin'?
Dont ye view dat ship a come a sailin'?
Dont ye view dat ship a come a sailin'? Hallelujah.
Dat ship is heavy loaded, Hallelujah,]
Dat ship is heavy loaded,
Dat ship is heavy loaded,
Dat ship is heavy loaded, Hallelujah.

2
Dat ship is heavy loaded, Hallelujah, &c.

3
She neither reels nor totters, Hallelujah.

4
She is loaded wid-a bright angels, Hallelujah.

5
Oh, how do you know dey are angels? Hallelujah.

6
I know dem by a de'r mournin', Hallelujah.

7
Oh, yonder comes my Jesus, Hallelujah.

8
Oh, how do you know it is Jesus? Hallelujah.

9
I know him by-a his shinin', Hallelujah.

I don't feel no-ways tired.

[I am seekin' for a city, Hallelujah,
seekin' for a city, Hallelujah,
city into de heaven, Hallelujah,
city into de heaven, Hallelujah.
Oh, bredren, trabbel wid me, Hallelujah,
bredren, trabbel wid me? Hallelujah,
will you go along wid me? Hallelujah,
will you go along wid me? Hallelujah.
Lord, I don't feel no-ways tired,
Children, Oh glory Hallelujah,
For I hope to shout glory when dis world is on fiah,
Children, Oh, glory Hallelujah.]

2
We will trabbel on together, Hallelujah, (*bis*)
Gwine to war agin de debbel, Hallelujah, (*bis*)
Gwine to pull down Satan's kingdom, Hallelujah, (*bis*)

Gwine to build up de walls o' Zion, Hallelujah. (*bis*)
CHO.--Lord, I don't feel no-ways tired, &c.

3
Dere is a better day a comin', Hallelujah, (*bis*)
When I leave dis world o' sorrer, Hallelujah, (*bis*)
For to jine de holy number, Hallelujah, (*bis*)
Den we'll talk de trouble ober, Hallelujah. (*bis*)
CHO.--Lord, I don't feel no-ways tired, &c.

4
Gwine to walk about in Zion, Hallelujah, (*bis*)
Gwine to talk a wid de angels, Hallelujah, (*bis*)
Gwine to tell God 'bout my crosses, Hallelujah, (*bis*)
Gwine to reign wid Him foreber, Hallelujah. (*bis*)
CHO.--Lord, I don't feel no-ways tired, &c.

Did you hear my Jesus.

Did you hear my Jesus.—*Concluded.*

[Ef you want to get to hebben, come along, come along,
Ef you want to get to hebben, come along, come along,
Ef you want to get to hebben, come along, come along,
Hear my Jesus when He call you.
Ef you want to see de angels, come along, come along,
Ef you want to see de angels, come along, come along,
Ef you want to see de angels, come along, come along,
Hear my Jesus when He call you.
Did you hear my Jesus when He call you,
Did you hear my Jesus when He call you,
Did you hear my Jesus when He call you,
For to try on your long white robe.]

2
Oh, de hebben gates are open, come along, come along,
Oh, de hebben gates are open, come along, come along, (*bis.*),
Hear my Jesus when He call you;
Oh, my mother's in de kingdom, come along, come along,
Oh, my mother's in de kingdom, come along, come along, (*bis.*),
Hear my Jesus when He call you,
I am gwine to meet her yander, come along, come along,
I am gwine to meet her yander, come along, come along, (*bis.*),
Hear my Jesus when He call you.

CHO.--Did you hear my Jesus when he call you,
Did you hear my Jesus when he call you, (*bis,*),
For to try on your long white robe.

3
Ef you want to wear de slippers, come along, come along,
Ef you want to wear de slippers, come along, come along, (*bis.*),
Hear my Jesus when He call you;
Ef you want to lib forever, come along, come along,
Ef you want to lib forever, come along, come along, (*bis.*),
Hear my Jesus when He call you;
Did you hear my Jesus calling, "come along, come along,"
Did you hear my Jesus calling, "come along, come along." (*bis.*),
Hear my Jesus when He call you.
CHO.--Did you hear my Jesus when He call you,
Did you hear my Jesus when He call you, (*bis.*),
For to try on your long white robe.

Zion, weep a-low.

Zion, weep a-low.—Concluded.

[Zion, weep a-low,
Zion, weep a-low,
Zion, weep a-low,
Den-a Hallelujah to-a de Lamb.
My Jesus Christ, a-walkin' down de hebbenly road,
Den a Hallelujah to-a de Lamb,
An' out o' his mouth come a two-edged sword,
Den a Hallelujah to-a de Lamb,
Say, what sort o' sword dat you talkin' 'bout
Den a Hallelujah to-a de Lamb,
I'm talkin' 'bout dat two-edged sword,
Den a Hallelujah to-a de Lamb. Oh.]

2
Oh, look up yonder, Lord, a-what I see,
Den a Hallelujah, &c.,
Dere's a long tall angel a comin' a'ter me,
Den a Hallelujah, &c.,
Wid a palms o' vicatry in-a my hand,
Den a Hallelujah, &c.,

Wid a golden crown a-placed on-a my head,
Den a Hallelujah, &c. CHO.--Oh, Zion, weep a-low.

3
Zion been a-weepin' all o' de day,
Den a Hallelujah, &c.,
Say, come, poor sinners, come-a an' pray,
Den a Hallelujah, &c.,
Oh, Satan, like a dat huntin' dog,
Den a Hallelujah, &c.,
He hunt dem a Christian's home to God,
Den a Hallelujah, &c. CHO.--Oh, Zion, weep a-low.

4
Oh, Hebben so high, an' I so low,
Den a Hallelujah, &c.,
I don' know shall I ebber get to Hebben or no,
Den a Hallelujah, &c.,
Gwine to tell my brudder befo' I go,
Den a Hallelujah, &c.,
What a dolesome road-a I had to go,
Den a Hallelujah, &c. CHO.--Oh, Zion, weep a-low.

Sweet Canaan.

My mother used to tell me how the colored People all expected to be free some day, and how one night, a great many of them met together in a Cabin, and tied little budgets on their backs, as though they expected to go off some where, and cried, and shook hands, and sang this hymn.

ALICE DAVIS.

[Oh, de land I am bound for,

Sweet Canaan's happy land I am bound for,
Sweet Canaan's happy land I am bound for,
Sweet Canaan's happy land,
Pray, give me your right hand.

Oh, my brother, did you come for to help me,
Oh, my brother, did you come for to help me,
Oh, my brother, did you come for to help me;
Pray, give me your right hand,

Oh, my sister, did you come for to help me,
Oh, my sister, did you come for to help me,
Oh, my sister, did you come for to help me;
Pray, &c.]

    NOTE.--There is so little variety to the verses of "Sweet Canaan" that we have not thought it worth while to give them at greater length. They readily suggest themselves, and seem to be limited only by the number of the singer's relations and friends.

In dat great gittin-up Mornin'.

THIS song is a remarkable paraphrase of a portion of the Book of Revelations, and one of the finest specimens of negro "Spirituals." The student who brought it to us, and who sings the Solos, has furnished all that he can remember of the almost interminable succession of verses, which he has heard sung for half an hour at a time, by the slaves in their midnight meetings in the woods. He gives the following interesting account of its origin:

"I have heard my uncle sing this hymn, and he told me how it was made. It was made by an old slave who knew nothing about letters or figures. He could not count the number of rails that he would split when he was tasked by his master to split 150 a day. But he tried to lead a Christian life, and he dreamed of the General Judgment, and told his fellow-servants about it, and then made a tune to it, and sang it in his cabin meetings."

J. B. TOWE.

In dat great gittin-up Mornin'.—Concluded.

[I'm a gwine to tell you bout de comin' ob de Saviour;
Fare-you-well, Fare-you-well.
I'm a gwine to tell you 'bout de comin ob de Saviour;
Fare-you-well, Fare-you-well.
Dar's a better day a comin';
Fare-you-well, Fare-you-well;
When my Lord speaks to His Fader;
Fare-you-well, Fare-you-well.
Says Fader, I'm tired o' bearin',
Fare-you-well, Fare-you-well.
Tired o' bearin for poor sinners;
Fare-you-well, Fare-you-well.
Oh, preachers, fold your Bibles;
Fare-you-well; Fare-you-well;
Prayer-makers pray no more;
Fare-you-well, Fare-you-well,
For de last soul's converted;
Fare-you-well, Fare-you-well;
For de last soul's converted;
Fare-you-well, Fare-you-well.
In dat great gettin-up Mornin;
Fare-you-well, Fare-you-well,
In dat great gittin-up mornin';
Fare-you-well, Fare-you-well.]

Hampton and Its Students

2. Dere's a better day a comin',

3. When my Lord speaks to his Fader,

4. Says, Fader, I'm tired o' bearin',

5. Tired o' bearin' for poor sinners,

6. Oh preachers, fold your Bibles,

7. Prayer-makers pray no more,

8. For de last soul's converted. (*bis*) *Cho*.

9. De Lord spoke to Gabriel.

10. Say, go look behind de altar,

11. Take down de silver trumpet,

12. Go down to de sea-side,

13. Place one foot on de dry land,

14. Place de oder on de sea,

15. Raise, your hand to heaven,

16. Declare by your Maker,

17. Dat time shall be no longer. (*bis*) *Cho*.

18. Blow your trumpet, Gabriel.

19. Lord, how loud shall I blow it?

20. Blow it right calm and easy,

21. Do not alarm my people,

Hampton and Its Students

22. Tell dem to come to judgment. (*bis*) *Cho*.

23. Den you see de coffins bustin',

24. Den you see de Christian risin',

25. Den you, see de righteous marchin',

26. Dey are marchin' home to heaven.

27. Den look upon Mount Zion,

28. You see my Jesus comin'

29. Wid all his holy angels.

30. Where you runnin', sinner?

31. Judgment day is comin'. (*bis*) *Cho*.

32. Gabriel, blow your trumpet,

33. Lord, how loud shall I blow it?

34. Loud as seven peals of thunder,

35. Wake de sleepin' nations.

36. Den you see poor sinners risin.

37. See de dry bones a creepin', *Cho*.

38. Den you see de world on fire,

39. You see de moon a bleedin',

40. See de stars a fallin',

41. See de elements meltin',

42. See de forked lightnin',

43. Hear de rumblin' thunder.

44. Earth shall reel and totter,

45. Hell shall be uncapped,

46. De dragon shall be loosened.

47. Fare-you-well, poor sinner. *Cho.*

48. Den you look up in de heaven,

49. See your mother in heaven,

50. While you're doomed to destruction.

51. When de partin' word is given,

52. De Christian shouts to your ruin.

53. No mercy'll ever reach you, *Cho.*

54. Den you'll cry out for cold water,

55. While de Christian's shoutin' in glory,

56. Sayin' amen to your damnation,

57. Den you hear de sinner sayin',

58. Down I'm rollin', down I'm rollin',

59. Den de righteous housed in heaven,

60. Live wid God forever. (*bis.*) *Cho.*

Walk you in de Light.

[Walk you in de light,
Walk you in de light,
Walk you in de light,
Walkin' in de light o' God, Oh, children.
Oh, children, do you think it's true,
Walkin' in de light o' God,
Dat Jesus Christ did die for you,
Walkin' in de light o' God,
Yes, He died for me an' He died for you,
Walkin' in de light o' God,
For de Holy Bible does say so,
Walkin' in de light o' God,]

2
I think I heard some children say,
Walkin' in de light o' God,
Dat dey neber heard de'r parents pray,
Walkin' in de light o' God.
Oh, parents, dat is not de way,
Walkin' in de light o' God,
But teach your children to watch an' pray,
Walkin' in de light o' God.
CHO.--Oh, parents, walk you in delight,
Walk you in de light, walk you in de light,
Walkin' in de light o' God.

3
I love to shout, I love to sing,
Walkin' in de light o' God,

I love to praise my Heavenly King,
Walkin' in de light o' God.
Oh, sisters, can't you help me sing,
Walkin' in de light o' God,
For Moses' sister did help him,
Walkin' in de light o' God.
CHO.--Oh, sisters, walk you in de light, &c.

4
Oh, de heavenly lan' so bright an' fair,
Walkin' in de light o' God,
A very few dat enter dere,
Walkin' in de light o' God.
For good Elijah did declare,
Walkin' in de light o' God,
Dat nothin' but de righteous shall go dere,
Walkin' in de light o' God.
CHO.--Oh, Christians, walk you in de light, &c.

Sweet Turtle Dove, or Jerusalem Mornin'.

Sweet Turtle Dove.—Concluded.

[1
Sweet turtle dove, she sing-a so sweet,
Muddy de water, so deep,
An' we had a little meetin' in de mornin',
A-for to hear Gabel's trumpet sound.
Jerusalem mornin', Jerusalem mornin' by de light,
Don't you hear Gabel's trumpet in dat mornin'?

2
Old sister Winny, she took her seat,
An she want all de members to foller her,
An' we had a little meetin' in de mornin',
A-for to hear Gabel's trumpet sound.]

2
Ole sister Hannah, she took her seat,
An' she want all de member to foller her;
An' we had a little meetin' in de mornin'
A-for to hear Gabel's trumpet sound.
CHO.--Jerusalem mornin', &c.

3
Sweet turtle dove, she sing-a so sweet,

Muddy de water, so deep,
An' we had a little meetin' in de mornin',
A-for to hear Gabel's trumpet sound.
CHO--Jerusalem mornin', &c.

(SOLO.) 5
Ole brudder Philip, he took his seat,
An' he want all de member to foller him,
An' we had a little meetin' in de mornin,'
A-for to hear Gabel's trumpet sound.
CHO.--Jerusalem, mornin', &c.

(SOLO.) 6
Ole sister Hagar, she took her seat,
An' she want all de member to foller her,
An' we had a little meetin' in de mornin',
A-for to hear Gabel's trumpet sound,
CHO.--Jerusalem mornin', &c.

(SOLO.) 7
Ole brudder Moses took his seat,
An' he want all de member to foller him,
An' we had a little meetin' in de mornin',
A-for to hear Gabel's trumpet sound.
CHO.--Jerusalem mornin', &c.

8
Sweet turtle dove, she sing-a so sweet,
Muddy de water. so deep,
An' we had a little meetin' in de mornin'.
A-for to hear Gabel's trumpet sound.
CHO--Jerusalem mornin', &c.

Gideon's Band; or, De milk-white Horses.

The explanation which has been given us of the origin of this curious hymn is, we think, invaluable as an example of the manner in which external facts grew to have a strange symbolical meaning in the imaginative mind of the negro race.

In a little town in one of the Southern States, a Scriptural panorama was exhibited, in which Gideon's Band held a prominent place, the leader being conspicuously mounted upon a white horse. The black people of the neighborhood crowded to see it, and suddenly, and to themselves inexplicably, this swinging "Milk-White Horses" sprang up among them, establishing itself soon as a standard church and chimney-corner hymn.

Hampton and Its Students

Gideon's Band.—Concluded.

[Oh, de band ob Gideon, band ob Gideon,
band ob Gideon, ober in Jordan,
Band ob Gideon, Band ob Gideon,
How I long to see that day.
Oh, de milk-white horses, milk-white horses,
milk-white horses, ober in Jordan,
milk-white horses, milk-white horses,
How I long to see that day.
I hail to my sister, my sister she bow low,
Say, don't you want to go to hebben,
How I long to see that day.
Oh, de twelve white horses, twelve white horses,
twelve white horses, ober in Jordan,
Twelve white horses, twelve white horses,
How I long to see that day.
Oh, hitch'em to the chariot, hitch'em to de chariot,
hitch' em to de chariot, ober in Jordan,

Hitch'em to the chariot, hitch'em to de chariot,
How I long, &c.]

2
DUO.--I hail to my brudder, my brudder he bow low,
Say, don't you want to go to hebben?--
How I long to see dat day!
CHO.--Oh, ride up in de chariot, ride up in de chariot,
Ride up in de chariot ober in Jordan;
Ride up in de chariot, ride up in de chariot--
How I long to see dat day!
It's a golden chariot, a golden chariot,
Golden chariot ober in Jordan;
Golden chariot, a golden chariot--
How I *long* to see dat day!

3
Duo.--I hail to de mourner, de mourner he bow low,
Say, don't you want to go to hebben?--
How I long to see dat day!
CHO.--Oh, de milk an' honey, milk an' honey,
Milk an' honey ober in Jordan;
Milk an' honey, milk an' honey--
How I long to see dat day!
Oh, de healin' water, de healin' water,
Healin' water ober in Jordan
Healin' water, de healin' water--
How I *long* to see dat day!

Hampton and Its Students

De Winter'll soon be Over.

[Oh, de winter, de winter, de winter'll soon be ober, children,
de winter, de winter, de winter'll soon be ober, children,

de winter, de winter, de winter'll soon be ober, children,
Yes, my Lord:
Oh look up yonder what I see,
Bright angels comin' arter me.]

2
I turn my eyes towards de sky,
An' ask de Lord for wings to fly;
If you get dere before I do,
Look out for me I'm comin' too. *Cho*.

3
Oh Jordan's ribber is deep an' wide,
But Jesus stan' on de hebbenly side;
An when we get on Canaan's shore,
We'll shout, an' sing forebber more. *Cho*.

Keep Me from sinkin' Down.

[Oh Lord, Oh my Lord! Oh my good Lord!

Hampton and Its Students

Keep me from sinkin' down, Oh my Lord.
Oh my good Lord, Keep me from sinkin' down.

I tell you what I mean to do,
Keep me from sinkin' down
I mean to go to hebben too,
Keep me from sinkin' down.

I bless de Lord I'm gwine to die.
Keep me from sinkin' down,
I'm gwine to judgment by an' by.
Keep me from sinkin' down.]

Hear de Angels singin'.

[Oh, sing all de way, sing all de way,
Sing all de way, my Lord,
Hear de angels singin'.
We're marchin' up to Hebben, its a happy time;
An' Jesus is on-a de middle line;
Dem-a Christians take up too much time;
Dey're idlin' on dat battle line;
Hear de angels singin'.]

2
Now all things well, an' I don't dread hell;--
Hear de angels singin',
I am goin' up to Hebben' where my Jesus dwell;--
Hear de angels singin'.
For de angels are callin' me away,--

Hear de angels singin',
An' I must go, I cannot stay,--
Hear de angels singin'. CHO.--Oh, sing, &c.

3
Now take your Bible, an' read it through,--
Hear de angels singin',
An' ebery word you'll find is true;--
Hear de angels singin'.
For in dat Bible you will see,--
Hear de angels singin',
Dat Jesus died for you an' me,--
Hear de angels singin'. CHO.--Oh, sing, &c.

4
Say if my memory sarves me right,--
Hear de angels singin',
We're sure to hab a little shout to-night,--
Hear de angels singin'.
For I love to shout, I love to sing,--
Hear de angels singin',
I love to praise my Hebbenly King,--
Hear de angels singin'. CHO.--Oh, sing, &c.

I've been a-list'ning all de Night long.

[I've been a list'ning all de night long,
Been a list'ning all de day,
I've been a list'ning all de night long,
To hear some sinner pray.
Some said that John, de Baptist,
Was nothin' but a Jew,

But the Bible doth inform us
Dat he was a preacher too.]

2.
Go, read the fifth of Matthew,
An' a read de chapter thro',
It is de guide to Christians,
An' a tells dem what to do.
CHO.--I've been a list'ning, &c.

3.
Dere was a search in heaven,
An' a all de earth around,
John stood in sorrow hoping
Dat a Saviour might be found.
CHO.--I've been a list'ning, &c.

Babylon's Fallin'.

This is often used in Hampton as a marching song, and is quite effective when the two hundred students are filing out of the assembly room to its movement. We recommend it for similar use to Schools and Kindergartens.

Babylon's Fallin'.—Concluded.

[Pure city, Babylon's fallin', to rise no more,
Pure city, Babylon's fallin', to rise no more,
Oh, Babylon's fallin', fallin', fallin',
Babylon's fallin' to rise no more,
Oh, Babylon's fallin', fallin', fallin',
Babylon's fallin' to rise no more.

Oh, Jesus tell you once before
Babylon's fallin' to rise no more;
To go in peace an' sin no more;
Babylon's fallin' to rise no more.
If you get dere before I do,
Babylon's fallin' to rise no more;
Tell all my friends I'm comin' too;
Babylon, &c.]

De ole Ark a-moverin' Along.

De ole Ark a-moverin' Along.

[Jes' wait a little while, I'm gwine to tell ye 'bout de ole ark
De Lord told Noah for to build him an ole ark,
De ole ark a-moverin', a-moverin' along,
Oh de ole ark a-moverin', a-moverin', a-moverin',
De ole ark a-moverin', a-moverin' along,
Ole ark a-moverin', a-moverin' along,

2
Den Noah an' his sons went to work upon de dry lan',
De ole ark, a-moverin', &c.,
Dey built dat ark jes' accordin' to de comman',
De ole ark a-moverin', &c.,
Noah an' his sons went to work upon de timber,
De ole ark a-moverin', &c.,
De proud began to laugh, an' de silly point de'r finger,
De ole ark a-moverin', &c.
CHO.--De ole ark a-moverin', &c.

3
When de ark was finished jes' accordin' to de plan,
De ole ark a-movering, &c.,
Massa Noah took in his family, both animal an' man,
De ole ark a-moverin, &c.,
When de rain began to fall an' de ark began to rise,
De ole ark a-moverin', &c.,
De wicked hung around' wid der groans an' de'r cries,
De ole ark a-moverin,' &c.
CHO.--Oh de ole ark a-moverin, &c.

4
Forty days an' forty nights, de rain it kep' a fallin',
De ole ark, a-moverin', &c.
De wicked clumb de trees, an' for help dey kep' a callin',
De ole ark a-moverin', &c.,
Dat awful rain, she stopped at last, de waters dey subsided,
De ole ark a-moverin', &c.,
An' dat ole ark wid all on board on Ararat she rided,
De ole ark a-moverin', &c.,
CHO.--Oh, de ole ark a-moverin, &c.

Hampton and Its Students

Dust an' Ashes.

Hampton and Its Students

Dust an' Ashes.

1.
[Dust, dust an' ashes fly over on my grave,
Dust, dust an' ashes fly over on my grave,
Dust, dust an' ashes fly over on my grave,
An' de Lord shall bear my spirit home,
An' de Lord shall bear my spirit home.

2.
Dey crucified my Saviour,
An' nailed Him to de cross,
Dey crucified my Saviour,
An' nailed Him to de cross,
Dey crucified my Saviour,
An' nailed Him to de cross,
An' de Lord shall bear my spirit home,

3.
Oh, Joseph begged His body,
An' laid it in de tomb,
Oh, Joseph begged His body,
An' laid it in de tomb,
Oh, Joseph begged His body,
An' laid it in de tomb,
An' de Lord shall bear, &c.

4.
De angel came from heaven,
An' roll de stone away,
De angel came from heaven,
An' roll de stone away,
De angel came from heaven,
An' roll de stone away,
An' de Lord shall bear, &c.

5.
De cold grave could not hold Him,
Nor death's cold iron band,
De cold grave could not hold Him,

Nor death's cold iron band,
De cold grave could not hold Him,
Nor death's cold iron band,
An' de Lord shall bear, &c.
An' de Lord shall bear my spirit home,
He rose, He rose, He rose from de dead,
He rose, He rose, He rose from de dead.
He rose, He rose, He rose from de dead,
an' de Lord shall bear my spirit home;
An' de Lord shall bear my spirit home.

6.
Oh Mary came a-runnin', her Saviour for to see,
Oh Mary came a-runnin', her Saviour for to see,
Oh Mary came a-runnin', her Saviour for to see,
An' de Lord shall bear my spirit home,
An' de Lord shall bear my spirit home.

7.
De angel say He is not here, He's gone to Galilee,
De angel say He is not here, He's gone to Galilee,
De angel say He is not here, He's gone to Galilee,
An' de Lord shall bear my spirit home,
An' de Lord shall bear my spirit home.
De angel say He is not here, He's gone to Galilee,
De angel say He is not here, He's gone to Galilee,
De angel say He is not here, He's gone to Galilee,
An' de Lord shall bear my spirit home,
An' de Lord shall bear my spirit home.

He rose, He rose, He rose from de dead,
He rose, He rose, He rose from de dead,
He rose, He rose, He rose from de dead,
An' de Lord shall bear my spirit home;
An' de Lord shall bear my spirit home.]

Hampton and Its Students

Hampton and Its Students

www.ingramcontent.com/pod-product-compliance
Lightning Source LLC
Chambersburg PA
CBHW081846170426
43199CB00018B/2829